PRAISE FOR *A CRASH COURSE IN SPSS FOR WINDOWS*

"Do you think SPSS manuals are generally far more cumbersome than they need to be? Do your students find learning SPSS for Windows from a manual a time-consuming ordeal? *A Crash Course in SPSS for Windows* enables students to learn the package quickly and painlessly, provided they have some background knowledge of statistics. Why use *A Crash Course in SPSS for Windows?* This clear, explicit and user-friendly text enables most users to learn the basics comfortably within ten hours and makes it enjoyable."

Gnist Akademika

"I have taken several classes that have used SPSS. When I started taking these classes I had little to no knowledge about statistics. It was extremely frustrating to under-stand the texts that were put out by SPSS. After reviewing this book, I have a clear understanding of how to use SPSS. It made the difficult task of understanding the output simple. SPSS is intuitive, in the sense that it is simple to pick a test and run it. However, understanding which particular piece of data is of interest to you is not intuitive. This book helps clear up the jungle of data that you have to trek through to come up with your conclusion."

Amazon.com reader

"Reading the book is made considerably easier due to its neat layout and a contents page which lets the reader turn to the appropriate section with ease. The chapters all have a cover page explaining what the chapter will include and when reading through the chapters the reader's eye is immediately drawn to the key points which are highlighted using a darker font. Bullet points allow the reader to follow the steps to figuring out the procedure with considerable ease and they are written in a way that is coherent and makes the process less complex.

With its spacious layout making it easy to read and the ring binder finish allowing pages to be accessed more effectively this book is successful in demonstrating how to use SPSS to interpret, analyse, and draw up results using a variety of different tests."

Marianne Bigg, BPS Student Rep.

"This textbook provides an inexpensive and quick way to become familiar with SPSS. True to its title, the book presents an abbreviated introduction to SPSS without being brusque. The authors expect novices to be able to complete the book in under 10 hours. For those familiar with the Windows operating system and spreadsheet programs (e.g., Excel), the material can completed in a few hours less . . . overall, the book delivers a quick and easy to follow introduction to SPSS suitable for novices."

J. Wade Davis in The American Statistician

D1515109

A Crash Course in SPSS for Windows

Fourth Edition Updated for Versions 14, 15, and 16

Andrew M. Colman and
Briony D. Pulford

A John Wiley & Sons, Ltd., Publication

This fourth edition first published 2008

© 2008 Andrew M. Colman and Briony D. Pulford

Edition history: Blackwell Publishing Ltd (1e, 2000; 2e 2003, 3e, 2006)

Blackwell Publishing was acquired by John Wiley & Sons in February 2007. Blackwell's publishing program has been merged with Wiley's global Scientific, Technical, and Medical business to form Wiley-Blackwell.

Registered Office

John Wiley & Sons Ltd, The Atrium, Southern Gate, Chichester, West Sussex, PO19 8SQ, United Kingdom

Editorial Offices

350 Main Street, Malden, MA 02148-5020, USA

9600 Garsington Road, Oxford, OX4 2DQ, UK

The Atrium, Southern Gate, Chichester, West Sussex, PO19 8SQ, UK

For details of our global editorial offices, for customer services, and for information about how to apply for permission to reuse the copyright material in this book please see our website at www.wiley.com/wiley-blackwell.

The right of Andrew M. Colman and Briony D. Pulford to be identified as the author of this work has been asserted in accordance with the Copyright, Designs and Patents Act 1988.

Wiley also publishes its books in a variety of electronic formats. Some content that appears in print may not be available in electronic books.

Designations used by companies to distinguish their products are often claimed as trademarks. All brand names and product names used in this book are trade names, service marks, trademarks or registered trademarks of their respective owners. The publisher is not associated with any product or vendor mentioned in this book. This publication is designed to provide accurate and authoritative information in regard to the subject matter covered. It is sold on the understanding that the publisher is not engaged in rendering professional services. If professional advice or other expert assistance is required, the services of a competent professional should be sought.

Library of Congress Cataloging-in-Publication Data

Colman, Andrew M.

A crash course in SPSS for Windows : updated for versions 14, 15, and 16 / Andrew M. Colman and Briony D. Pulford. — 4th ed.

p. cm.

Includes bibliographical references and index.

ISBN 978-1-4051-8402-1 (pbk. : alk. paper) 1. SPSS for Windows. 2. Social sciences—Statistical methods—Computer programs. I. Pulford, Briony. II. Title.

HA32.C63 2008

519.50285′53—dc22

2008017213

A catalogue record for this book is available from the British Library.

Set in 10/12pt Galliard by Graphicraft Limited, Hong Kong
Printed in Singapore by Markono Print Media Pte Ltd

1   2008

Contents

Preface to the Fourth Edition

With the help of this *Crash Course*, you should be able to learn SPSS quickly and painlessly, provided that you have some background knowledge of statistics. SPSS is not hard to use, and we can explain the basics to you without fuss. In our experience, busy people dislike spending large amounts of time learning computer applications. We believe that most SPSS manuals are far more cumbersome than they need to be. Learning SPSS with more conventional manuals is time-consuming and quite an ordeal.

This book is designed to make things quicker and easier. It grew out of a specific need, and it proved popular because it filled a gap in the market, although since the first edition, some flattering imitations have appeared in print. Almost all computational examples in our *Crash Course* are taken from real data in published research, rather than hypothetical examples such as are found in most statistics and computing books, but we have chosen small data sets to spare you the time and boredom involved in inputting data.

The contents and presentation of the book were greatly improved by usability trials that we carried out for the first edition. We sent a rough draft of the book to 15 students and academics at a dozen different universities, all of whom had expressed a wish to learn SPSS but had no previous knowledge or experience of it, and we asked them to work through the course carefully, making notes of everything that they found unclear or felt could be improved, and keeping a record of the time taken to complete the course. The results were enormously helpful. Our readers came up with comments, criticisms, and useful suggestions for every chapter. These responses enabled us to produce a revised version incorporating a vast number of improvements, big and small, and we know of no other SPSS manual that has had the benefit of such systematic feedback from the end-users for whom it is intended. The time taken to complete the course in the usability trials ranged from five and a half to nine hours, with a mean of just under seven hours (6 hours 52 minutes, to be exact), usually spread over several sessions. The content has expanded slightly since then, but most readers should still be able to complete the course within about 10 hours.

The first two chapters are written with complete beginners in mind. They describe the basic features of SPSS and explain from the very beginning how to get it up and running. If you already have some familiarity with Windows-based applications, then we suggest that you just skim these introductory chapters, but do make a note of the less familiar information in sections 2.3 and 2.4. Chapter 3 describes how data are loaded and printed in SPSS, and this will also be fairly familiar territory to many readers. The remaining chapters describe the most widely used statistical techniques and graphic facilities available in SPSS.

Most of the procedures covered in this book are included in the SPSS Base System. The exceptions are repeated-measures analysis of variance (chapter 11) and log-linear analysis (chapter 13), both of which are supplied with the SPSS Advanced Models add-on module, which has to be purchased separately. If you don't have the Advanced Models module, then you'll have to skip those chapters.

The first edition of the *Crash Course*, published in 2000, was designed for use with versions 8 and 9 of SPSS for Windows. The second edition, published in 2003, was for versions 10 and 11, and the third edition, published in 2006, was for versions 10 to 13. The changes for the second and third editions were largely matters of detail, but there were many of them. In almost every paragraph, small alterations had to be made to accommodate changes in SPSS from earlier versions. Because we are very explicit about exactly which keys to press, even minor alterations necessitated textual changes. For the second edition, in response to requests from readers, we also added two completely new chapters, chapter 13 on log-linear analysis and chapter 14 on factor analysis, and for the third edition, we added chapter 16 on handling variables and large data files, chapter 17 on syntax windows, and a short appendix on exporting and importing Excel files.

This fourth edition became necessary because of further minor modifications introduced in SPSS versions 14, 15, and 16. The procedures themselves have remained largely unchanged, but various alterations to the Data Editor, Output Viewer, Chart Editor, and dialog boxes mean that a user running SPSS 14, 15, or 16 cannot always follow the key strokes precisely as set out in earlier editions. We have deleted some very elementary material on using Windows, because Windows applications are now so well known. We've added a brief comment on splitting files to chapter 4 and, at the suggestion of a colleague, a section on partial correlations to chapter 5. We've added lots of useful SPSS procedures, including sorting, classifying, and coding data, inserting variables and cases, and paneling charts and graphs. Throughout the book, we've rewritten passages to improve clarity and readability.

The earlier editions of this *Crash Course* were well received by readers, many of whom have been in touch with us, and there's been a steady demand for it throughout the English-speaking world. But there's always room for further improvement, and we believe that this edition represents a significant leap forward.

We're grateful to everyone who took part in the usability trials, and to others who have offered technical advice and help of various kinds. In particular, we wish to express our gratitude to Joseph Amoah-Nyako, John Armstrong, John Beckett, Sarah Bird, Mark Bowers, Kenneth Cowley, Simon Dunkley, Joanne Emery, Sarah Fishburn, Gerry Gardner, Kate Garland, Erica Grossman, Rob Hemmings, Richard Joiner, Geoff Lowe, Sandy MacRae, Rhonda Pearce, Ian Pountney, Caroline Salinger,

Berni Simmons, Kathy Smith, Helga Sneddon, Jonathan Stirk, David Stretch, Catherine Sugden, Johnny Sung, Carolyn Tarrant, Cathy Thorp, Gary van Heerden, Stephen L. White, Sue Wilson, and Alison Wray. We also wish to acknowledge the support of the University of Leicester in granting us study leave, during which we prepared the latest edition of this book.

We've made the book as straightforward as possible, but not totally idiot-proof, partly because that wouldn't have been possible and partly because only an idiot would want to read an idiot-proof book. But we've done our best to make it clear, explicit, and user-friendly, and we'd appreciate hearing from students and researchers about any further improvements that might be worth introducing into future editions. We'll acknowledge everyone who offers helpful suggestions unless they ask us not to. Feel free to e-mail us directly about the contents or presentation of the book, or write to us care of the publisher, but please don't ask us for statistical help or advice on how to analyse your data.

Andrew Colman (amc@le.ac.uk)
Briony Pulford (bdp5@le.ac.uk)

Online support material to accompany this text is available at
http://www.blackwellpublishing.com/crashcourse

Choosing an Appropriate Statistical Procedure

- **Purpose of statistical analysis**
  - **Summarizing univariate data**
    - Descriptive statistics (mean, standard deviation, variance, etc.)
  - **Exploring relationships between variables**
    - **Form of data**
      - **Frequencies** → Number of variables
        - One: compared to theoretical distribution → Chi-square goodness-of-fit test
        - Two: tested for association → Chi-square test of association
        - Multiple: tested for association → Log-linear analysis
      - **Measurements** → Number of variables
        - Two: degree of linear relationship → Level of measurement
          - Ordinal → Spearman's rho
          - Interval → Pearson's correlation coefficient
        - Multiple: effect of 2+ predictors on a dependent variable → Multiple regression
        - Multiple: factors underlying correlation matrix → Factor analysis
  - **Testing significance of differences**
    - **Number of groups**
      - One: mean compared to a specified value → One-sample t test
      - **Two**
        - Independent samples → Form of data
          - Ordinal → Mann–Whitney U test
          - Interval → Independent-samples t test
        - Related samples → Form of data
          - Ordinal → Wilcoxon matched-pairs test
          - Interval → Paired-samples t test
      - **Multiple**
        - Independent samples
          - One independent variable → One-way ANOVA
          - Multiple independent variables → Multifactorial ANOVA
        - Related samples → Repeated-measures ANOVA

WHERE TO FIND THINGS IN SPSS

Procedure	Menu location
Analysis of variance	*See* Multifactorial analysis of variance, One-way analysis of variance, Repeated-measures analysis of variance
ANOVA	*See* Multifactorial analysis of variance, One-way analysis of variance, Repeated-measures analysis of variance
Charts and graphs	Graphs Chart Builder . . .

Chi-square goodness-of-fit test	Analyze
	    Nonparametric Tests
	        Chi-Square . . .

Chi-square test of association	Analyze
	    Descriptive Statistics
	        Crosstabs . . .

Correlation	*See* Partial correlation, Pearson's correlation coefficient, Spearman's rho

Descriptive statistics	Analyze
	    Descriptive Statistics
	        Frequencies . . . /Descriptives . . . etc.

Factor analysis	Analyze
	    Data Reduction
	        Factor . . .

Goodness of fit	*See* Chi-square goodness-of-fit test
Graphs	*See* Charts and graphs

Independent-samples t test	Analyze
	    Compare Means
	        Independent-Samples T Test . . .

Log-linear analysis	Analyze
	    Loglinear
	        Model Selection . . .

Mann–Whitney U test	Analyze
	    Nonparametric Tests
	        2 Independent Samples . . .

Matched-groups t test	*See* Paired-samples t test

Mean	Analyze
	    Descriptive Statistics
	        Descriptives . . .

Multifactorial analysis of variance	Analyze
	    General Linear Model
	        Univariate . . .

Where to Find Things in SPSS

Procedure	Menu location

Multiple regression	Analyze
	    Regression
	        Linear . . .

One-sample *t* test	Analyze
	    Compare Means
	        One-Sample T Test . . .

One-way analysis of variance	Analyze
	    Compare Means
	        One-Way ANOVA . . .

Paired-samples *t* test	Analyze
	    Compare Means
	        Paired-Samples T Test . . .

Partial correlation	Analyze
	    Correlate
	        Partial . . .

Pearson's correlation coefficient	Analyze
	    Correlate
	        Bivariate . . .

Related-groups *t* test	*See* Paired-samples *t* test

Repeated-measures analysis of variance	Analyze
	    General Linear Model
	        Repeated Measures . . .

Rho	*See* Spearman's rho

Spearman's rho	Analyze
	    Correlate
	        Bivariate . . .

Standard deviation	Analyze
	    Descriptive Statistics
	        Descriptives . . .

t test	*See* Independent-samples *t* test, One-sample *t* test, Paired-samples *t* test
U test	*See* Mann–Whitney *U* test

Variance	Analyze
	    Descriptive Statistics
	        Descriptives . . .

Wilcoxon matched-pairs test	Analyze
	    Nonparametric Tests
	        2 Independent Samples . . .

Wilcoxon signed-ranks test	*See* Wilcoxon matched-pairs test

1 Introduction

When SPSS Inc. of Chicago, Illinois, USA was founded in 1968, the letters SPSS stood for Statistical Package for the Social Sciences. Later, as the company grew beyond its purely academic roots, this was changed to Statistical Product and Service Solutions. Today, the company uses SPSS as a name and no longer as an abbreviation for something else. The detailed operations described in this book apply specifically to versions 14, 15, and 16, and the screenshots are from version 15. For earlier versions of SPSS, there are slight variations, but most of the essential features remain the same. In version 16, most of the buttons are the same as in versions 14 and 15, but some are transposed, so the ones that appear in the screenshots on the right-hand side are now along the bottom, and those on the bottom are now down the right.

SPSS is the oldest and most popular of the many packages of computer programs currently available for statistical analysis. Although it's extremely powerful, it's relatively easy to use once you've been taught the rudiments. We can teach you the rudiments quite quickly, and you'll certainly need our guidance, because the package is not self-explanatory and you cannot simply teach yourself to use it just by fiddling around and using the help menu, as one of us was annoyed to discover long ago. For both of us, and many people we've spoken to, the chief problem in learning to use it is that the various manuals on the market – some issued by SPSS Inc. and many more by independent writers – are too detailed, too complicated, and above all too *long* to provide the quick introduction that we need. This book is aimed at readers like ourselves who lack the time to plough through thick manuals, or the patience to submit to a screen-based tutor, but who want to be able to pick up the essential skills for performing standard statistical analyses with SPSS, and who prefer to learn these skills rapidly and painlessly. If you are one of those people who *are* happy to spend many evenings and weekends learning SPSS the long way, then our considered advice to you is that you should get out more and develop some new leisure activities.

Chapter 2 will focus on the essential information that you need for getting started. If you're already familiar with Windows, then you only really need to read sections 2.3 and 2.4. The chapters that follow will tell you how to load data, how to print results, how to obtain descriptive statistics, including means, standard deviations, and variances, how to compute Pearson's correlation coefficient, partial correlations, Spearman's rho, chi-square tests, t tests for independent and paired samples, Mann–Whitney U tests, Wilcoxon matched-pairs tests, analysis of variance in all its major forms, multiple regression, log-linear analysis, and factor analysis, how to draw charts and graphs, how to change and create variables, how to handle data files, and how to work with SPSS syntax windows. The statistical procedures covered by this book include the most important ones used by psychologists and other social and beha-vioural scientists. Once you've mastered these techniques, you should have little difficulty teaching yourself other procedures available in SPSS.

This book will not teach you statistics. We assume that you already know enough about statistics to understand what assumptions are made about the data that you enter into SPSS, what procedures to use for analysing the data, and how to interpret the results. There's no point trying to analyse data unless you know what you're doing. If you need to brush up on your statistics, there are many good books for you to consult. Among the ones that we're happy to recommend are Hays (2007), Howell (2008), Huck (2008), Norman and Streiner (2008), and Pagano (2007). (Biblio-graphical details can be found in the list of references at the back of this book.) We have, none the less, included very brief introductions to the essential ideas behind the statistical procedures at the beginning of most chapters, and in the preliminary pages there's a flow chart to help you choose an appropriate statistical procedure and a table showing where to find things in SPSS. The flow chart and table are restricted to the most commonly used procedures specifically dealt with in this book. There are far more statistical procedures available in SPSS, and both the flow chart and the table are only rudimentary, in the spirit of the book as a whole.

Even if you know what you're doing, the output that you obtain will be of little value if your data are of poor quality. This nugget of truth is expressed in the com-puter slang word *gigo*, which stands for *garbage in, garbage out*. Awesome though it is, SPSS is not a magic oven that can miraculously transform garbage input into *haute cuisine* output. To get useful output, you need properly collected data and carefully considered statistical analysis.

We hope and expect that this book will put you on the road to becoming a fluent and efficient SPSS data analyst. Believe it or not, data analysis is fun, once you get the hang of it. Our usability trials, referred to in the preface, suggest that our *Crash Course in SPSS for Windows* should not take more than about 10 hours and that most people find it quite enjoyable. Happy computing!

2 Using Windows

2.1 RUNNING SPSS

We're going to show you how to use SPSS from scratch, but the first thing to do after switching on your computer and its monitor (screen) is to run the SPSS statistics package. How you do this depends on how your computer has been configured. When the computer is switched on, it will probably boot up directly into the Windows desktop, with little graphic icons representing various applications, including SPSS, and a **Start** button in the lower-left corner of the window. Once Windows is running, and the screen shows the Windows desktop, there are two main ways of running SPSS.

1 If the Windows desktop displays an SPSS icon (pictured), you can launch the program directly with the mouse, by double-clicking the icon. Eventually, SPSS will be up and running, and you'll know that it is because the SPSS Data Editor will appear. From now on, whenever we refer to the mouse button without saying which one, we'll mean the left-hand mouse button, and whenever we refer to clicking, we'll mean pressing this mouse button.

2 The other method of launching SPSS, and the one you'll have to use if the SPSS icon isn't visible on the desktop, is as follows. Move the mouse pointer on to the **Start** button in the lower-left corner, and click once. Alternatively, if you have a Windows keyboard, you may press either of the Windows keys near the space bar. In the pop-up list that appears, use the mouse or the keyboard cursor keys to highlight **All Programs** (or **Programs**), and then slide the mouse pointer across to the submenu of programs on the right and highlight **SPSS**. Now slide across to the sub-submenu and highlight **SPSS 15.0** (or **SPSS 14.0**, or whatever the version is).

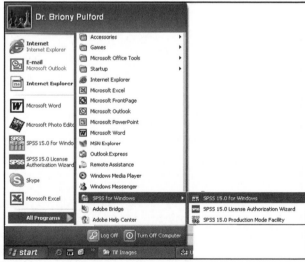

With **SPSS 15.0** (or another version) highlighted, either click the mouse or press the ENTER key. This will start the program running, and after a few seconds you will see the SPSS Data Editor.

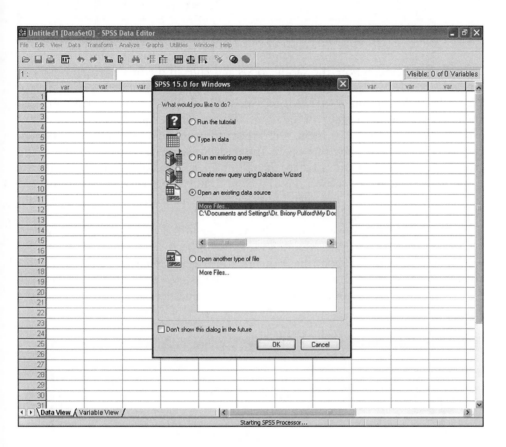

Depending on how the program is configured on your computer, a dialog box may appear in front of the Data Editor, asking you "What would you like to do?" and listing various options. If this dialog box appears, click the radio button next to **Type in data**, because you haven't yet got an existing data source, and then click the **OK** button at the bottom of the dialog box. Later on, you'll select **Open an existing data source**. Round buttons of this type are called radio buttons because, like the buttons on a car radio, only one can be selected at a time. If you put a tick in the check box labelled **Don't show this dialog in the future**, by clicking the check box, then the "What would you like to do?" dialog box will not reappear.

The SPSS Data Editor is divided into rows and columns and is captioned (in its title bar at the top) **Untitled1 [DataSet0] – SPSS Data Editor**. Immediately below the title bar is a menu bar.

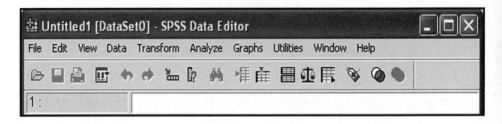

For the time being, ignore the various odds and ends in the menu bar and the icon bar immediately below it. Hold the mouse pointer over each of the icons in turn to read a brief description of it; we'll tell you what they are as and when you need them. Notice the word **Help** on the right. You can click it with the mouse whenever you like, and a drop-down menu will appear from which you can choose **Topics**, and then in the dialog box that opens **Index** or **Search** to look something up. You may also use click the **Contents** tab, then double-click the book symbol, or click the + sign next to it, to see subsections. To close a subsection, click the – sign next to the book, or double-click the open book. Click the small cross in the box's top-right corner to close the help system.

Many of the dialog boxes that you'll encounter in the chapters that follow have specialized help buttons that are often more useful because they're context-specific: they supply information about the particular job you are doing at the time. Feel free to click the **Help** button whenever you feel helpless, or even just curious. You can always close the **Help Topics** box that opens box and get back to where you were before by clicking the small cross in the box's top-right corner.

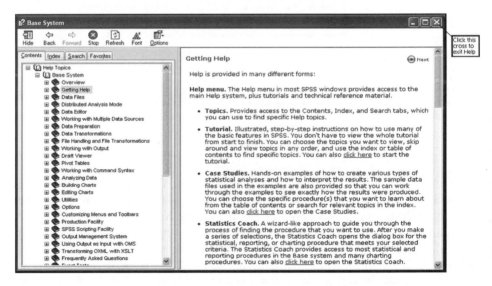

If at any time you open a dialog box or a sub-dialog box and make changes that you don't want to keep, or if you enter a dialog box and then wish you hadn't, then just click the **Cancel** button or the cross in the red box in the top-right corner of the dialog box and you will close it without any changes being saved.

2.2 RESIZING AND MOVING A WINDOW

Now we'll show you how to resize and move a window. First of all, to alter the size of a window, click one of the buttons that appear in the title bar near the top-right corner of most windows:

◆ To *minimize* a window – that is, to reduce it to a tiny icon at the bottom of the window without closing it – click the small dash on the left. Try it now, and after minimizing the window, restore it by clicking its icon, labelled **Untitled1[DataSet0] – SPSS Data Editor**, in the task bar at the bottom of the Windows desktop. If you are have lots and lots of windows open, then you may have to click the SPSS icon at the bottom of the window and then select the window that you want to see from the list that pops up above it.

◆ To *reduce* the size of a currently active window and reveal any other working windows lurking behind it, click the overlapping rectangles in the middle (top right corner of the window). Try it now, and notice how the Data Editor window is reduced in size, revealing the Windows desktop in the background. This is the only other working window, because you haven't done any analysis or drawn any charts or graphs yet.

◆ You can *move* a window across the screen to a new position, but this is possible only if it has first been reduced. Click its title bar and hold the mouse button down instead of releasing it. With the mouse button held down, drag the mouse until the window is where you want it to be, and then release the button. Try moving the reduced Data Editor window now.

Notice that when you reduced the size of the Data Editor window, the middle resizing button changed from overlapping rectangles to a single rectangle:

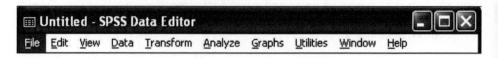

♦ To *maximize* a window that has been reduced – to restore it so that it fills the whole screen – click the rectangle in the middle. Restore the Data Editor to its full size now.
♦ If you wanted to *close* the window and shut down the program, then you could click the red box with the cross, but don't do it now, because we have more to tell you about the Data Editor.

2.3 THE DATA EDITOR

As long as the Data Editor window is active, you can enter data into SPSS. We'll give you a small data set to enter by hand. The scores come from a well-known Danish study of the IQ scores of 12 pairs of identical twins separated early in life and raised in different homes (Juel-Nielsen, 1965).

> *Twin A:* 119, 99, 108, 91, 111, 105, 100, 91, 104, 125, 111, 99
> *Twin B:* 121, 103, 97, 100, 117, 97, 94, 98, 103, 111, 117, 112

To compute any statistics for this data set, you must first enter the scores into the Data Editor, which is essentially a spreadsheet – an array of rows and columns extending downwards and to the right, far beyond what you can see on the screen. Its rows are labelled **1**, **2**, **3**, and so on, and its columns are all initially labelled **var** (short for variable). For some types of analysis in SPSS, data must be set out with each group of scores, or each variable, in a separate column. For other types of analysis, the data must be arranged in a single column, with one score per row, even if they come from two or more groups. We'll return to this complication in section 6.2. For now, we'll show you how to enter the 12 pairs of IQ scores in the natural way, in two separate columns.

The first column will contain the IQ scores labelled *twina*, and the second column the scores labelled *twinb*. Beginning at the beginning, the first column will contain, from top to bottom, the numbers 119, 99, 108, and so on, and the second column will contain 121, 103, 97, and so on. The data will be set out as shown in the screenshot once you have keyed them into the Data Editor.

TWINSIQ.sav - SPSS Data Editor

File Edit View Data Transform Analyze

1 : twina   119

	twina	twinb	V
1	119.00	121.00	
2	99.00	103.00	
3	108.00	97.00	
4	91.00	100.00	
5	111.00	117.00	
6	105.00	97.00	
7	100.00	94.00	
8	91.00	98.00	
9	104.00	103.00	
10	125.00	111.00	
11	111.00	117.00	
12	99.00	112.00	

You should first name the variables so that the output is properly labelled and understandable.

◆ Click the **Variable View** tab at the bottom-left of the Data Editor. A window will appear in which the variables are numbered 1, 2, and so on down the left, and the columns are headed **Name**, **Type**, **Width**, and so on.

◆ The first row of the first column, headed **Name**, should appear as the active cell, highlighted with a dark border round it. If for any reason it isn't, then select that cell by clicking inside it. Once it is active, type **twina** inside it, then move to the second row of the same column, either with the mouse or the cursor keys, and type **twinb**. Variable names can be up to 64 characters long and have capitals or lower-case letters but no other characters, no spaces, and no numbers at the start. Earlier versions of SPSS were limited to eight characters for variable names, and if you intend to transfer the data set to another machine or user, then restricting variable names to eight letters may be advisable.

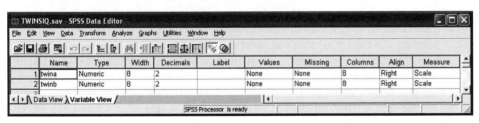

TWINSIQ.sav - SPSS Data Editor

File Edit View Data Transform Analyze Graphs Utilities Window Help

	Name	Type	Width	Decimals	Label	Values	Missing	Columns	Align	Measure
1	twina	Numeric	8	2		None	None	8	Right	Scale
2	twinb	Numeric	8	2		None	None	8	Right	Scale

Data View \ Variable View /

SPSS Processor is ready

The various other columns in the Variable View window are for specifying special properties of variables. By clicking in each column of the **twina** or **twinb** row, and then clicking the grey area or scroll box that appears on the right-hand side of the cell, or in the case of **Label** by simply typing in the cell, you can change the width of the column, change the default number of decimal places, label the variable, specify missing data, and so on. Under **Missing**, you can specify a number such as 999 to be treated by SPSS as a missing data item. Pick a number for the missing data that would not naturally occur in your data and that stands out as obviously not a real score. Blank cells are treated as missing data automatically, but sometimes you want to use a particular code to show that a missing item is not a data entry mistake or different codes to represent different categories of missing data. But for our current purposes (and in practice most straightforward analyses) the defaults are fine, so just ignore the other columns at this stage.

♦ Now that you have finished naming both variables, click the **Data View** tab at the bottom of the window to get back to the data input window of the Data Editor. Notice that the first two columns are now headed **twina** and **twinb**.

2.4 ENTERING DATA

You can type your raw scores directly into the cells of the Data Editor, or you can type them in an area called the cell editor just below the Data Editor's icon bar and transfer them to the cells below by pressing ENTER. The score will then jump into the active cell – the one that is currently highlighted with a black border.

♦ Before entering the first number, make sure that the correct cell, namely **1:twina**, is active (highlighted). To highlight it, simply click inside it.
♦ Use the number keys at the top of the keyboard. You may prefer to use the numeric keypad on the right, in which case make sure that the number lock (Num Lock) is on. If you're using a laptop computer, it probably won't have a numeric keypad. Enter the first score from the Twin A group, which happens to be **119**, by typing it into the cell or into the cell editor and then pressing ENTER (note that we use **Courier bold** font for anything that you need to type). The score will align itself in the first cell and the highlight will move to the next cell down. You could enter the score 99 here, because that is the second score from the Twin A group.
♦ Depending on the order in which you want to enter the data, you may find it more convenient to press one of the cursor keys rather than ENTER after typing a number into the cell editor. For example, after typing the first score, if instead of pressing ENTER you press the right-pointing cursor key, then the first number will be transferred to the first row of the first column exactly as before, but the next cell to be highlighted will be the one immediately to the right of it (**1:twinb**), where you could enter **121** (the first score from the Twin B group) before moving on to the second row, where the next pair of IQ scores need to be entered. Use whichever method suits you best.
♦ Use the cursor keys to move around the Data Editor if you find yourself in the wrong place. If at any point you find that the wrong cell is active, you can highlight the correct one simply by clicking inside it.

◆ If after entering some or all of the data, you find that you have made a mistake, highlight the offending cell, and then simply enter the new number in the cell editor and press ENTER. The new entry will replace the old. To delete the contents of any cell, highlight the cell and press the DELETE (Del) key. To delete a whole column, click the grey area at the top of the column where its name appears, so that the whole column is highlighted, and then press the DELETE key. You can highlight and delete a whole row in the same way, by clicking in a numbered row of the grey border on the left. If at any time you notice that you have accidentally created too many rows and the ones at the bottom are empty, and are just showing dots indicating missing data, then you should delete those empty rows so that they don't show up on your output as missing data.

◆ To insert a new blank case or variable into your data set (other than at the end of existing data), click to highlight the row where you want the new case and click **Edit** then **Insert Cases**, or highlight the column where you want the new variable, then click **Edit** then **Insert Variables**. By selecting/highlighting multiple rows or columns you can use this to insert several cases or variables at once.

◆ You may want to move rows or columns around to organize your data set. For example, with a large data set, you may want to put the most important variables first. To do this, move the cursor to the grey area at the top of the column where its name appears, then click, so that the whole column is highlighted, and drag it to its new position. A red line will appear between the columns as you move about to show where the column will go when you release the mouse button. Several columns can be moved at once by selecting them together using click and hold and then dragging the selected columns.

2.5 SCROLLING

As you enter data, the Data Editor will fill up, and if you have more data than can fit in the rows and columns of the window, then some of the data may scroll out of sight. For example, some of the data that you entered in section 2.4 may have scrolled off the top of the window if you have a small screen. If you need to examine data that have disappeared from view, you can do this either with the cursor keys or the mouse.

◆ *Using the cursor keys.* To see information that has scrolled off the top of the window, press the **up** cursor key, and the hidden information will reappear. To scroll down again, press the **down** cursor key. You may also scroll to the left and right by using the **left** and **right** cursor keys, but no left–right scrolling is necessary with the data you have just entered because there were not enough columns for anything to have scrolled off to the left.

◆ *Using the mouse.* The right-hand border of the Data Editor is actually a scroll bar – this is a standard feature of most Windows applications.

At the top and bottom of the scroll bar are arrows pointing up and down respectively, and between the two is a slider bar that is activated when some information has disappeared from view. To scroll, click the slider bar and, with the mouse button held down, drag the slider bar up or down, then release the mouse button, and the display will scroll, assuming that there are some data off the screen to scroll to. This is a slightly awkward manoeuvre, and there's another slower but easier method. Click the scroll arrow at the top or bottom of the scroll bar, and the display will scroll up or down. There is a similar scroll bar with its own scroll arrows and slider bar in the bottom border of the Data Editor, and it can be used in exactly the same way for scrolling to the left or right if there are enough columns of input data to have caused the display to have scrolled off to the left.

2.6 CUTTING AND PASTING

For certain analyses discussed in later chapters of this book, you'll have to format the data with all of the scores in a single column, one score per row, and with a separate column containing a grouping variable indicating the group to which each score belongs. There are many other circumstances in which you may need to cut and paste. We'll show you now how to cut and paste the input data so that all the IQ scores are in a single column.

◆ Select the 12 scores in the second column, labelled **twinb**, either by clicking and dragging or clicking and shift-clicking (see section 3.3 if this is unfamiliar to you).
◆ Click **Edit** in the menu bar.

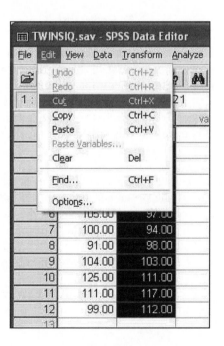

◆ In the Edit drop-down menu that appears, click **Cut**. The **twinb** scores will vanish.
◆ Select the next empty cell (row 13) below the **twina** scores in the first column of the Data Editor.
◆ Click **Edit** in the menu bar once more, but this time choose **Paste** from the drop-down Edit menu that appears. The scores from Group 2 will be pasted into the **twina** column.
◆ Now, just to get used to it, cut and paste the bottom 12 scores in rows 13 to 24 back into the second column, where they originally came from. After selecting and using **Edit**, then **Cut**, click the empty cell in row 1 below the **twinb** label, and **Paste**. If you don't want to use the drop-down Edit menu for cut and paste then you could alternatively use either the right mouse button to select the cut, copy, or paste functions, or use Ctrl+X, Ctrl+C, or Ctrl+V respectively.
◆ Notice that rows 13 to 24 have dots in them. SPSS thinks there are missing data in those empty cells. Click the row number 13 in the left margin, to highlight the whole of row 13, then hold down the Shift key and click the row number 24 in the left margin. Now rows 13 to 24 are highlighted. Delete these rows by clicking **Edit** in the menu bar, followed by **Cut** or by pressing the **Delete** key on your keyboard. The rows with dots in them will disappear, and you will be back to where you were before you pasted data into those rows.

You can of course also use the above procedure to copy and paste data without deleting the original data. To do this select **Copy** instead of **Cut**.

2.7 SAVING DATA

Having entered data into SPSS, you will often want to save the data for future analysis or re-analysis. Depending on the machine you're using, you may or may not be able to save the data on the computer's hard drive, but you can normally save a file on a USB flash memory stick instead. This is generally more convenient, because you can take it away with you, so we'll show you how to do that.

◆ First, make sure that the data you want to save are in the Data Editor.
◆ Insert the memory stick into a USB port.
◆ Click the word **File** in the menu bar near the top of the Data Editor. A drop-down file menu will appear.

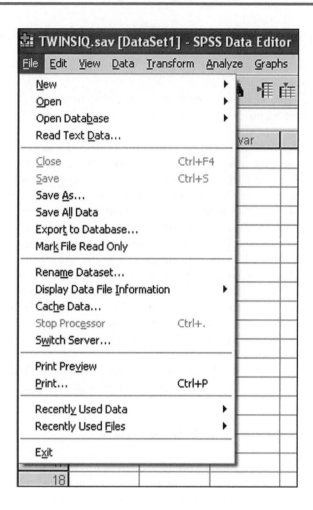

◆ Provided that the Data Editor has some data in it, the command **Save As...** will be shown in black. Menu items that are dimmed – displayed tantalizingly in light grey – are currently unavailable. Use the mouse or the cursor arrows to highlight **Save As...**, then click it, and a dialog box called Save Data As will appear. It's worth pointing out that an SPSS menu command followed by three dots always opens a dialog box, and a menu command followed by an arrowhead always opens a submenu.

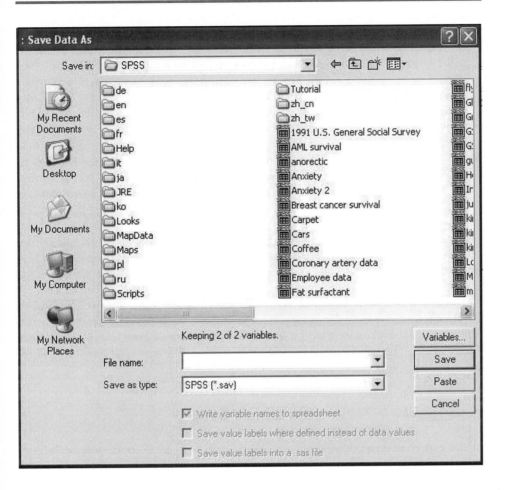

◆ Now tell the computer on which drive to save your data. By default, the list box labelled **Save in** near the top of this dialog box will probably be showing **SPSS**, but you're not going to save your data in the default folder on the computer's hard drive. Click the black arrow on the right of the list box, and a drop-down list will appear. Alternatively click the **My Computer** icon on the left of the screen. Use the mouse or the cursor arrows to highlight the memory stick, which will be labelled as **Removable Disk (E:)** (the letter may be different) and click it or press the ENTER key so that it appears in the **Save in** list box.

◆ Next, give the file a name. Click in the text box labelled **File name**, and type a suitable file name. A file name must begin with a letter but the first part need not be restricted to eight characters, as in earlier versions of SPSS, and it may now include spaces. A file name normally ends with a full stop and a three-letter extension, which in the case of an SPSS input data file should be **.sav**. A filename (one word) is the first part of a file name, without the extension. We suggest that you use the file name **twinsiq.sav**.

◆ Make sure that the list box labelled **Save as type** is showing **SPSS(*.sav)**. If it isn't, then click the black arrow on the right of the list box, and a drop-down list will appear. Use the mouse or the cursor arrows to highlight **SPSS(*.sav)**, and click it or press the ENTER key so that it appears in the list box. This ensures that your data will be saved in SPSS format. If you did want to save it in another format (for example, to show to someone whose machine doesn't have SPSS) then you could select a different format here, the most useful ones being Excel or tab-delimited.

◆ To save the file, click the **Save** button in the dialog box and wait for the data to be saved before removing your memory stick. Save the file now, because you'll need to retrieve it for chapters 3 and 4 – saving it at this point will mean that you won't have to key the data in again later.

You may notice that sometimes an asterisk appears in the top title bar, just before your data set name. This indicates that you have changed the data set since it was last saved and that you should resave it before shutting down, if you want to keep the changes.

If, when you have done some statistical analyses, you want to save the output file, then follow the same procedure as for saving data sets, the only difference being that you should make sure that the list box labelled **Save as type** is showing **Viewer Files(*.spo)**. The file name normally ends with a full stop and the three-letter extension **.spo**, in the case of an SPSS output file.

2.8 EXITING SPSS

At the end of your work session, you should exit from SPSS in an orderly fashion, unless you want to continue with the next chapter, in which case see below. You can exit via the **File** drop-down menu.

◆ Click **File** in the menu bar near the top of the Data Editor.

◆ Click **Exit** at the bottom of the menu. If you haven't saved your data, a dialog box will appear asking you whether you want to save the contents of the Data Editor. You should click **Yes** and save your data under the file name **twinsiq.sav**, as described in section 2.7, and exit SPSS, or exit directly if you have saved the information previously, in which case no dialog box will appear.

Alternatively, clicking the red box with the white cross in the top right corner of the Data Editor window (if it is the *only* Data Editor window open) will also close the whole SPSS programme down, whereas clicking it in an output or syntax window will only close that one window down.

3 Loading Data and Printing

3.1 LOADING DATA

It is not always necessary to key in data by hand. If you have a data file stored on disk or memory stick, sent to you via e-mail, or accessible from a web site, you can load it directly into SPSS for analysis. All the data sets used in this book can be downloaded from the Wiley-Blackwell publisher's web site for this book if you need them. Here's how to load the input data from chapter 2 into the Data Editor. First, run SPSS in the usual way from Windows desktop (see section 2.1), if it's not running already. When SPSS starts up, the Data Editor window will initially be active. Then do one of the following.

♦ If the "What would you like to do?" dialog box that we showed you in section 2.1 appears in front of the Data Editor, then click the radio button beside **Open an existing data source**, then click **OK**.

♦ Alternatively, if all you see is the Data Editor, then do it the long way. Click **File** in the menu bar near the top of the Data Editor. Another way of opening any of the menus in the menu bar, without using the mouse, is by pressing the Alt key and then typing the letter in the menu bar that is underlined – in this case **F**. In versions earlier than SPSS 13, these letters are permanently underlined, and you don't have to press the Alt key first. We'll usually show the underlined letters in this book – if you can't see them on your screen but want to use them, then just press Alt.

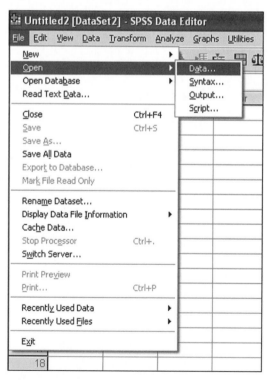

◆ If you used the dialog box and selected **Open an existing data source**, you'll already have the Open File dialog box. But if you're doing it the long way from the File menu, then select the command **Open** with the mouse, then click **Data...** in the submenu, and the Open File dialog box will appear. (Another tip: you can always execute a menu or submenu command by simply typing its underlined letter, in this case the letter **O** followed by **a**, *without* pressing the Alt key again.)

◆ Assuming that the data you want to load are on the USB drive, go to the list box labelled **Look in**. The list box will show either the default SPSS folder or the last folder that was opened in SPSS on this computer. Open the drop-down menu by clicking the arrow on the right of the list box, and click **Removable Disk (E:)** in the list of options displayed. The list box will now show the contents of **Removable Disk (E:)**. If your data were stored on the hard drive (C:) or another drive, you would, of course have selected the appropriate drive instead of E:. Navigate through the folders until you find the one where you stored the data set.

◆ Select the file you want by clicking its name in the Open File dialog box, which lists all SPSS data files with the extension **.sav**. If you had a long list of SPSS data files, you might have to use a scroll bar to see them all (see section 2.5). If your data file is not an ordinary SPSS data file, then you must specify something different in the **Files of type** list box, but we needn't go into that now (for an explanation of how to import Excel files, see Appendix 2 at the end of the book). The filename under which you saved the data in chapter 2 was **twinsiq**, and it was obviously a bog standard SPSS data file, so it should appear in the list. Select it by clicking it, and it will appear in the **File name** text box below.

◆ Once you are satisfied that you have selected the right file from the right drive, click **Open**. The Data Editor will reappear with your data from chapter 2 loaded into it, exactly as if you had just entered the scores by hand. If for some reason you didn't save the file earlier, then at this point you should go back to sections 2.3 and 2.4 and key the data in by hand.

One thing to note is that once you've opened a SPSS file on your computer it will usually appear in the **Recently Used Data**, or **Recently Used Files**, submenus, which will save you navigating around folders to locate it in future. If it's a data set you want to open, then look in the **Recently Used Data** submenu, and if you are looking for output files or syntax files, then look in the **Recently Used Files** submenu. If you are using a shared computer and haven't opened your personal SPSS files on it before, then these submenus won't have these quick links to your files. The Recently Used File List usually stores the last nine files viewed on the computer; this setting can be changed in the **General** tab of the **Options** dialog box in the **Edit** menu if needed.

Another thing that has changed from earlier versions of SPSS is that in versions 14, 15, and 16 it is possible to open more than one data set window at a time. Previously, it was only possible to have one data set open, which had to be saved and closed before a new one was opened. Having multiple data sets open at once can be useful if you are transferring or comparing data, but you should be mindful when running analyses which data set they are being performed on. This is especially true if two open data sets contain variables with the same names. To help you identify which data set is active, you should look at the taskbar at the bottom of the window where you will see the names of the open files (either side-by-side if the screen width allows it, or stacked one above another if you have a lot of files open). The active file has a green plus sign in the icon to the left of the filename. If you see two green plus signs, then one is indicating the active data set and the other indicates the active Output Viewer. To move between viewing different windows you can either click these file names in the taskbar, or you can use the drop-down list under **Window** in the menu bar at the top of the window. The analyses you perform will run on the active (green plus sign) data set and be put into the active (green plus sign) output file. All in all, to avoid confusion, it is much easier to have only one data set and one output file open at a time if you are new to SPSS!

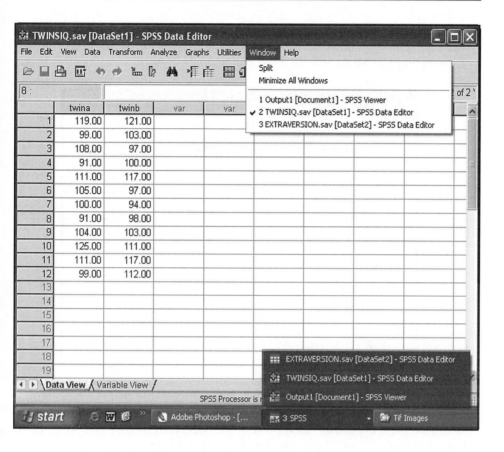

3.2 PRINTING AN ENTIRE DATA SET

At some stage you are bound to want to print a hard copy of some SPSS data. You may want to print input data from the Data Editor or, after you have analysed some data, you may want to print the results of your analysis from the Output Viewer, where the results are displayed. Your computer will, of course, have to be connected to a suitable printer. What to do if the set-up is wrong is beyond the scope of this *Crash Course*. Seek help. If a suitable printer is connected, then here's how to print your data. The procedure is essentially the same whether you are printing input or output data, so for now we'll print the input data that you currently have in the Data Editor, because you haven't any output results yet, though you'll have some soon, we promise.

◆ Make sure that your data file is in the Data Editor.
◆ If you want to see what your printing will look like, before you print it, then open the **File** drop-down menu by clicking its name in the menu bar, then click the command **Print Preview**. If you are happy with how it looks then click the **Print...** button to open the Print dialog box shown below.

◆ If you haven't gone through the "Print Preview" route just mentioned, then open the **File** drop-down menu by clicking its name in the menu bar, then click the command **Print...**, and the Print dialog box will open.

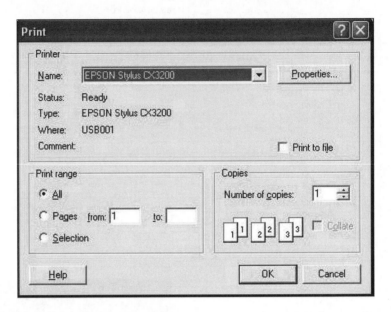

◆ To print the entire contents of the Data Editor, make sure that the radio button marked **All** is lit up. If it isn't, click it. The name of the printer displayed in the dialog box will depend on what printers are connected to your computer: using the drop-down menu, choose the one that you want to print to.
◆ Click **OK**, and the data will be printed. Try it now.

You can, if you wish, specify multiple copies of the printout by clicking the arrows on the right of the list box labelled **Number of copies**, but the default of one copy is what you'll usually want. If you're particularly fussy about the appearance of your printed data set – for example, if you want it to be in a certain font or with certain margin sizes or colour on it – then an easy option is to save the file in Excel format and then edit and print it from the Excel software. See Appendix 2 for information on how to transfer your data set into Excel.

3.3 PRINTING A SELECTION OF DATA

There may be times when you need to print only some of the input or output data in an SPSS window. To print a selection of the data that you have in the Data Editor, proceed as follows.

◆ Select the data that you want to print by either the click-and-drag or the click and shift-click technique. Suppose you want to print just the scores in the second column. Place the mouse pointer on the first of the **twinb** scores, press the mouse button and hold it down while dragging the mouse pointer over the rest of the scores in that column, and only then release the mouse button. The **twinb** scores will be highlighted in black – perhaps we should say lowlighted – apart from the first cell in the column, which was the active cell and is thus highlighted with a black border. You may find it easier to achieve the same effect by clicking the first score at the top of the **twinb** column, then holding down the Shift key (⇑) and clicking the bottom score in the column. The selected block of data will be highlighted. If you find that you've made a mistake and selected something you didn't intend to, then just click in an empty part of the Data Editor outside the marked block, and the highlight will vanish. Select some of the input data of twins' IQ scores now.

♦ Open the **File** drop-down menu by clicking its name in the menu bar, then click the command **Print...**, and the Print dialog box that we showed you before will appear.

♦ To print just the selected data in the active window, select the radio button marked **Selection** by clicking it.

♦ Click **OK**, and the selected data will be printed out for you.

♦ If you want to exit from SPSS at this stage, click **File** in the menu bar near the top of the Data Editor, followed by **Exit** at the bottom of the menu (see section 2.8). You'll be needing the twins' data again in chapter 4, so if you didn't save the file before, then when a dialog box appears inviting you to save the data, click **Yes** and save the file under the file name **twinsiq.sav** (see section 2.7). If you want to go straight on to the next chapter, then don't exit. Keep the data in the Data Editor.

4 General Descriptive Statistics

4.1 ANALYSING DATA

Now at last we're ready for some actual data analysis. We'll begin with general descriptive statistics, then in later chapters we'll move on to correlations and inferential statistics. Descriptive statistics are ways of summarizing numerical data to make them more easily interpretable, including especially the mean, standard deviation, variance, minimum, maximum, range, sum, standard error of the mean, kurtosis, and skewness of a set of scores. Correlations between variables are also descriptive statistics, strictly speaking, but they are treated separately by most statisticians (because they're not univariate), and chapter 5 will be devoted to them.

To calculate general descriptive statistics, you obviously need a set of data entered in the Data Editor. To save time and conserve energy, we suggest that you use the data that you saved in chapter 2 under the file name **twinsiq.sav**. If you're continuing straight from chapter 3, the data will be in the Data Editor. If you've restarted SPSS, the Data Editor window will be active, but without the twins data. There are two ways of proceeding at this point.

◆ If the familiar "What would you like to do?" dialog box has opened in front of the Data Editor, then click the radio button beside **Open an existing data source**, then click **OK**.

◆ If the dialog box has not appeared, then click **File** in the menu bar near the top of the Data Editor, select **Open**, click **Data** in the submenu, and follow the procedure described in section 3.1 to load **twinsiq.sav**. If you still haven't saved this file, then go to sections 2.3 and 2.4 and key the data in by hand.

4.2 MEANS, STANDARD DEVIATIONS, AND OTHER MEASURES

Once the twins data are in the Data Editor, you can calculate, for each group, the mean, standard deviation, minimum, and maximum, and if you wish you can also calculate the sum, variance, range, standard error of the mean, kurtosis, and skewness of each group. This is how you do it.

◆ Click **Analyze** in the menu bar near the top of the Data Editor. A drop-down menu will appear. Select the **Descriptive Statistics** command on this menu.

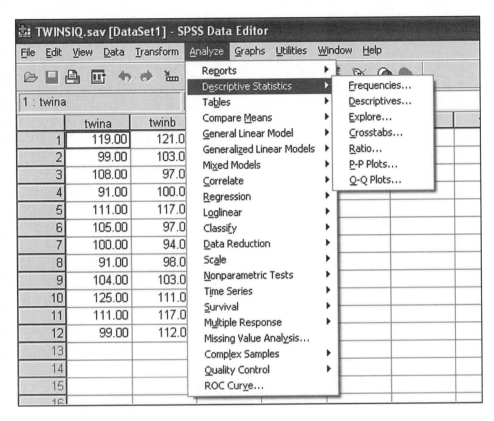

◆ When the Descriptive Statistics submenu opens, click **Descriptives...**, and try to remember for next time that this is where to find basic descriptive statistics in SPSS. The Descriptives dialog box will open.

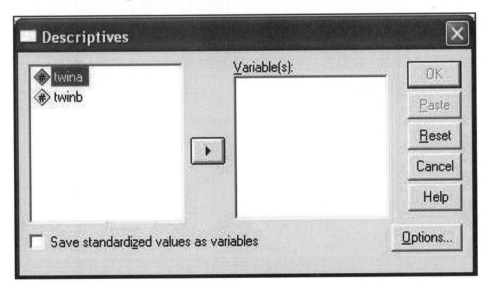

◆ In the Descriptives dialog box, the names of the variables in the data set are listed on the left, and on the right there is a box labelled **Variable(s)**. First move each of the variables for which you want descriptive statistics into the **Variable(s)** box by clicking its variable name to highlight it and then clicking the black arrow button pointing towards the **Variable(s)** box. The selected variable will shoot across into the **Variable(s)** box. Alternatively, you can double-click a variable and it will move to the **Variable(s)** box without the need to click the arrow button. It is also possible to hold the mouse button down and drag downwards to select many different variables and then press the black arrow button in the middle. If you make a mistake and want to move a variable back where it came from, then just select it in the right-hand box by clicking it and then click the arrow button, which will now obligingly be pointing to the left. Clicking the **Reset** button at any time will restore all variables to their original places, and all settings to their default values. For now, select both variables for analysis.

◆ If you wanted SPSS to convert the scores to standardized Z scores and to save them in that form, as new variables in the data editor, you could at this point click the check box beside **Save standardized values as variables**. This option is selected when a tick appears in its check box, and you can remove the tick by clicking again. There is no need for Z scores now.

◆ Click **Options...** at the bottom of the Descriptives dialog box to open a sub-dialog box in which you can specify which descriptive statistics to calculate.

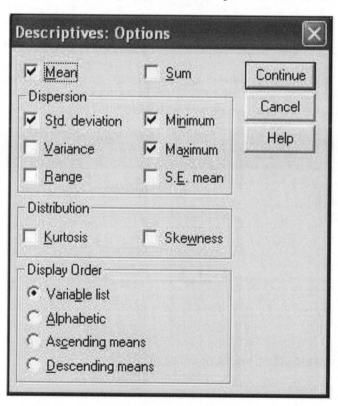

◆ When the sub-dialog box entitled Descriptives: Options opens, the options **Mean**, **Std. deviation** (standard deviation), **Mi_n_imum**, and **Ma_x_imum** are already selected by default, as shown by ticks in the check boxes alongside them. If you wished, you could select also **_S_um**, **_V_ariance**, **_R_ange**, **S._E_. mean** (standard error of the mean), **_K_urtosis**, and **Ske_w_ness** by clicking their check boxes or typing the corresponding underlined letters. It is also possible in the same dialog box to select the order in which the output results are displayed if this is important to you.

◆ Once you are satisfied that the options you want (for now, just the mean, standard deviation, minimum, and maximum), and only those, have been selected, click **Continue**. This will return you to the Descriptives dialog box.

◆ Now click **OK**, and after a pause the Output Viewer will appear with the results. The descriptive statistics for each of the groups that you included in the analysis will be displayed separately.

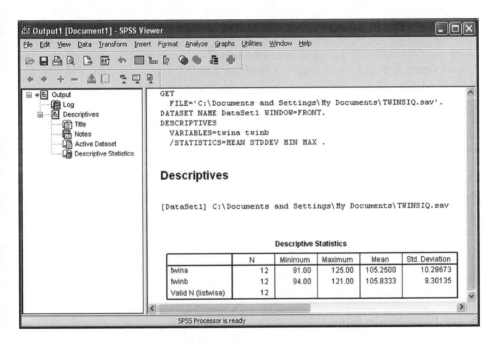

In the Output Viewer, a panel on the left shows the various elements of the output. You can go straight to any element by clicking its name in the left-hand panel. This is especially useful when the data fill more than a single screen. You can also hide any element of the output by clicking the minus sign in the box beside its name in the left-hand panel. The minus sign turns into a plus sign, and the corresponding element disappears from the output display on the right. If you click the plus sign, the output reappears. Similarly, to hide or show smaller parts of the output you can double-click the open or closed book symbols in the left-hand panel. You can reduce the size of the panel on the left, and simultaneously increase the area given over to displaying the actual output, by moving the mouse pointer to the right-hand border of the panel, when its arrowhead will turn into a double line with arrows, then pressing and holding down the mouse button and dragging the border to the left. This is useful when viewing large tables of output.

In the right-hand panel the output is displayed, but above the statistics that you want there are the Log (in SPSS versions 15 and 16) and the Active Dataset text box, both of which contain information about which data set was used to generate the analysis. These have been introduced into SPSS since it became possible to open multiple data sets at once (as mentioned in section 3.1), and helps reduce confusion. You can hide or show the Log and Active Dataset information, if you want to, by double-clicking the open or closed book symbols next to their names in the left-hand panel. The Log information (in SPSS 15 and 16, but not in version 14) also keeps a record of the syntax that you used to generate the analysis that you just ran (see Chapter 17 for an explanation of what syntax is). Fuller details about data sets, filters, missing cases, syntax, and the date of the analysis, for each analysis, can also be seen by double-clicking the closed book symbol, with the red letter **i** on it, next to Notes in the left-hand panel. If you want to stop the Log appearing each time you run an analysis, then you need to turn this function off in the **Edit** menu, by going to **Options** and opening the **Viewer** tab, where you can then change the **Initial Output State** on the left to **Hidden** for the Log, or untick the **Display commands in the log** box to just stop the syntax from appearing.

The output is self-explanatory. For example, although they were separated early in life and raised in different homes, the Twin A and Twin B groups have almost identical mean IQs of 105.25 and 105.83, respectively. To print a hard copy of the output, click **File** in the menu bar at the top of the Output Viewer, then **Print...**, and the descriptives output will be printed for you. What is printed out will depend on whether you selected **All visible output** (everything in the Output Viewer) or **Selection** (only the parts you selected in the output).

4.3 PASTING OUTPUT INTO A WORD DOCUMENT

You can copy and paste input data from the Data Editor and output from the Output Viewer into a Microsoft Word document, to include in a written report, for example. The procedure is quite simple, but not very satisfactory, because the variable names disappear and have to be reinserted by hand.

If you're determined to paste input data directly into a Word document in spite of our lack of enthusiasm, select the data, click **Edit** in the menu bar near the top of the Data Editor, then **Copy** then, without closing SPSS, open a Word document in the usual way, click **Edit**, then **Paste**, and the data from the Data Editor will be pasted into the Word document, but without the variable names. Try it with your twins input data.

There is a much better way of doing this. Appendix 2 explains how to export SPSS input data into a Microsoft Excel spreadsheet, and from Excel you can cut and paste the data much more efficiently and cleanly into a Word document, without losing the variable names. That's how we recommend you paste input data into Word. For output results, you can use the following procedure.

◆ Select all the output results by clicking **Output** in the panel on the left. (You could, if you wish, select just some of it by clicking its name in the left-hand panel or using the shift-click method for more than one item.)
◆ Click **Edit** in the menu bar at the top of the Output Viewer, then **Copy objects**, because what you are about to copy is not ordinary text.
◆ Get back to the Word document by clicking **Document1 – Microsoft Word** at the bottom of the window.
◆ Make sure the cursor is in the right place below the input data. Click **Edit** in the menu bar at the top of the Word window, followed by **Paste**.

The output results from the Output Viewer will be pasted into the Word document with the tables formatted as pictures, which can be moved or resized as necessary. If you wanted to edit the tables in Word, then you should select **Copy** rather than **Copy Objects**, and this would paste the output results as an editable Word table that you could then go on to change aspects such as borders, fonts, numbers, and so on. See Appendix 2 for further ways to export output to other software packages.

4.4 SPLITTING FILES

Sometimes you may want to look at the results of your statistical analyses for different groups of participants separately. For example, you may want to see if the correlation between x and y is stronger for men than for women, requiring the analysis to be carried out for these two groups separately. We can't show you how to do this with the data you currently have in the Data Editor, because it doesn't have a suitable splitting variable, but this is something that you may well want to come back to or look up at some point, because it's often very useful. If you turn on the Split File function you can then run *any* type of analysis and have the output separated by the grouping variable that you choose (e.g., gender).

To do this, you'd have to go to **Data**, then **Split File** before performing your statistical analysis, and in the dialog box that would then open, you'd choose either **Compare groups** (to show the output for each group in the same table when you do an analysis) or **Organize output by groups** (to show the output for each group in a separate table). A box labelled **Groups Based on:** would then become active, and you would select your splitting variable (such as gender) and move it to this box. Then, when you clicked **OK**, your file would sort itself according to your grouping variable, and subsequent analyses would all be split by this variable. You can group by more than one variable, if you like; for example, you could split by audience (three groups) and also gender (two groups) and thus have output showing results for all six groups.

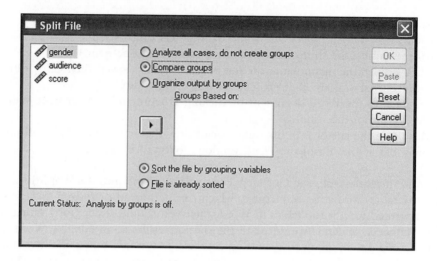

Something to bear in mind is that once you've turned this function on, it remains on for all the analyses you do until you go back to the Split File dialog box and click the button next to **Analyze all cases, do not create groups**, followed by **OK**.

◆ If you want to exit from SPSS at this point, then click **File** in the menu bar near the top of the Output Viewer, followed by **Exit** at the bottom of the menu that drops down (see section 2.7). A dialog box will appear asking you whether you want to save the contents of the Output Viewer. You may save the output in the usual way if you wish, or just click **No**. If you haven't already saved the data currently in the Data Editor, then another dialog box will appear inviting you to save these data, and you should click **Yes** and save them under the file name **twinsiq.sav**. If you want to go straight on to the next chapter, click **File** in the menu bar and select **New**, then click **Data** in the submenu and, once again, save the input data in the Data Editor if you haven't saved them already and a dialog box appears.

5 Correlation Coefficients

5.1 BACKGROUND

In statistics, the correlation between two variables is the degree of (usually) linear relationship between them, such that high scores on one tend to go with high scores on the other and low scores on one with low scores on the other (positive correlation), or such that high scores on one tend to go with low scores on the other (negative correlation). The concept of the correlation coefficient was first introduced by Sir Francis Galton in London in 1877. There are many different correlation coefficients, including coefficients of nonlinear correlation, but the most common are Pearson's product-moment correlation and Spearman's rho. Both of these coefficients range from −1.00 for perfect negative linear correlation, through zero for no linear correlation, to 1.00 for perfect positive linear correlation.

The most widely used index of all is Pearson's product-moment correlation coefficient. When social scientists refer to a correlation or a correlation coefficient without specifying the type, it is usually safe to assume that they are referring to Pearson's. Spearman's rho is a nonparametric version of Pearson's, designed for use with ordinal (ranked) data. In fact, from a mathematical point of view, Spearman's rho amounts to Pearson's product-moment correlation coefficient calculated after replacing the original scores by the ranks. Section 5.2 will describe the procedure for calculating Pearson's product-moment correlation coefficient, and section 5.4 will outline how to calculate Spearman's rho.

5.2 PEARSON'S CORRELATION COEFFICIENT

Hovland and Sears (1940) analysed some unusual data in their research into the relationship between frustration and aggression. They compared the annual number of lynchings that took place in the southern United States from 1882 to 1930 with the value of cotton production in the corresponding years. They hypothesized that lynchings could be viewed as acts of displaced aggression that should be more numerous during periods of economic hardship for farmers in the cotton-producing southern states, when cotton production was low, than during periods of prosperity, when cotton production was high. The data are shown in Table 5.1.

◆ If you've just restarted SPSS and the "What would you like to do?" dialog box has opened in front of the Data Editor, then click the radio button beside **Type in data**, followed by **OK**.

◆ Name two variables by clicking the **Variable View** tab at the bottom-left of the Data Editor and, in the first two rows of the **Name** column, type the names **cotton** and **lynch**, then click the **Data View** tab to return to the data entry window and enter the values of cotton production into the first column and the numbers of lynchings into the second column. (If you've forgotten how to name variables or how to enter data, then read sections 2.3 and 2.4 again.)

Table 5.1 Cotton production and lynchings

Year	Cotton ($m)	Lynchings	Year	Cotton ($m)	Lynchings
1882	310	49	1907	614	60
1883	251	52	1908	589	93
1884	254	52	1909	688	73
1885	270	80	1910	810	65
1886	257	74	1911	750	63
1887	291	73	1912	787	61
1888	292	70	1913	863	50
1889	308	95	1914	549	49
1890	350	90	1915	631	54
1891	313	121	1916	1122	50
1892	268	155	1917	1566	36
1893	264	155	1918	1738	60
1894	259	134	1919	2020	76
1895	293	112	1920	1069	53
1896	292	80	1921	676	59
1897	319	122	1922	1116	51
1898	305	102	1923	1454	29
1899	325	84	1924	1561	16
1900	438	107	1925	1577	17
1901	381	107	1926	1121	23
1902	422	86	1927	1308	16
1903	576	86	1928	1302	10
1904	561	83	1929	1245	7
1905	557	61	1930	659	20
1906	640	65			

◆ Save the input data for future reference by following the procedure described in section 2.7. Call the file **lynch.sav**.
◆ Click **Analyze** in the menu bar near the top of the SPSS Data Editor. Select **Correlate** in the drop-down menu that appears.

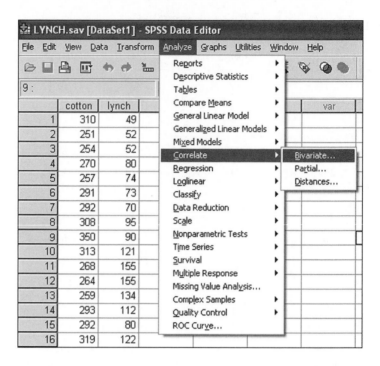

◆ Click **Bivariate...** in the submenu. This is the option for ordinary correlations between pairs of (bi-)variables. You could also have chosen **Partial...** for calculating partial correlations, which we'll show you in section 5.3. Or you could have chosen **Distances...** if you wanted to calculate various indices of similarity, dissimilarity, or distance. When you choose **Bivariate...**, the Bivariate Correlations dialog box will open.

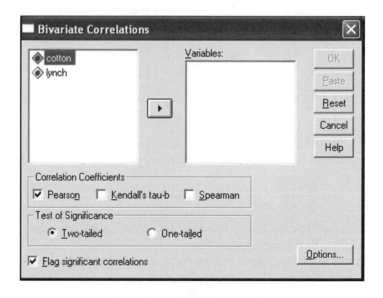

◆ The two variables that you have named **cotton** and **lynch** appear in the left-hand source box. Move **cotton** and **lynch** to the right-hand box, which is labelled **Variables**, by clicking each of them in turn and then clicking the black arrow button between the two boxes. (If you've forgotten how to do this, review section 4.2.)

◆ In the same dialog box, make sure that the type of correlation coefficient you want, namely **Pearson**, is selected. It is the default, but if for any reason the check box beside it doesn't have a tick inside it, click the check box. Make sure also that **Kendall's tau-b** and **Spearman**, which are nonparametric correlation coefficients, are deselected – if there are ticks in the check boxes beside them, click the boxes to remove the ticks. It is possible to choose more than one of the correlation coefficients if you wish, and that is why they have check boxes rather than radio buttons, but we're concentrating on Pearson's for the moment. We'll show you how to calculate Spearman's rho in section 5.4.

◆ Still in the Bivariate Correlations dialog box, select the test of significance you want to be applied to the correlation coefficient. **Two-tailed** is the default, but you could choose **One-tailed** if you wished by clicking its radio button. In order to cause correlation coefficients significant at the 0.05 level to be flagged with a single asterisk and coefficients significant at the 0.01 level with a double asterisk, make sure there's a tick in the check box beside **Flag significant correlations**. If this option is deselected (without a tick in its check box), then the output will still indicate the numerical values of the correlation coefficient and its significance level but will not asterisk the correlation if it is significant.

◆ The dialog box has a button labelled **Options...**, and if you clicked it, a sub-dialog box would open in which you could instruct SPSS to calculate means, standard deviations, cross-product deviations, and covariances. You would also be able to select a method of dealing with missing values, if you had any. The system default for handling missing values is to exclude cases pairwise; that is, to exclude from the calculation any cases (rows) with a missing value in either column.

◆ When you are satisfied that everything in the Bivariate Correlations dialog box is as you want it to be, click the **OK** button, and the Output Viewer will appear, displaying the results.

◆ If you want to print a hard copy of the output, follow the procedure described in section 3.2.

Correlations

Correlations

		cotton	lynch
cotton	Pearson Correlation	1	-.636**
	Sig. (2-tailed)		.000
	N	49	49
lynch	Pearson Correlation	-.636**	1
	Sig. (2-tailed)	.000	
	N	49	49

**. Correlation is significant at the 0.01 level

The output, headed **Correlations**, consists of a table showing the results of the Pearson correlation coefficient calculation. The results are in the form of a 2×2 matrix of numbers, but all you are interested in is the correlation between the value of cotton production and lynchings in the upper-right corner of the matrix or, what amounts to the same thing, the correlation between lynchings and the value of cotton production in the lower-left corner. The correlation of each variable with itself, which is given as 1.000, is about as interesting and informative as $1 \times 1 = 1$. The correlation of a variable with itself is inevitably 1.000. If you were studying the correlations between three variables, then the output would show a 3×3 matrix of bivariate correlations, and so on – SPSS can handle very large correlation matrices.

In this case, Pearson's product-moment correlation coefficient is $-.636$ or, as it is usually written, correct to two decimal places, $r = -.64$. The two-tailed significance of this correlation is .000, which does not mean exactly zero but means less than .001 ($p < .001$), and the number of cases is 49 ($N = 49$). Hovland and Sears (1940) got the same result, although they were working before the dawn of the computer age and must have calculated the correlation coefficient by hand.

In a journal article or research monograph, we would report these results as follows: "A large negative correlation was found between the annual number of lynchings that took place in the southern United States from 1882 to 1930 and the value of cotton production in the corresponding years, $r(47) = -.64$, $p < .001$ (two-tailed)." Note that if you are writing the results in this style, then you report the degrees of freedom, which are 47 because $df = n - 2$. An alternative way to report the correlation results is "$r = -.64$, $n = 49$, $p < .001$ (two-tailed)".

We described the correlation as "large" because, according to a widely accepted classification, a correlation of $r = .10$ represents a small effect size, $r = .30$ a medium effect size, and $r = .50$ a large effect size (see Cohen, 1992). It is clear that there was a large and significant negative correlation between the two variables in this study. It is also worth commenting that the square of a product-moment correlation coefficient indicates the degree of variance shared by the two variables, or the degree to which one explains the other. In this case, we can say that the two variables share more than 40 per cent of their variance in common, or that more than 40 per cent of the variance in lynchings is explained by the variance in cotton production values, because $-.64$ squared equals .41. In line with Hovland and Sears's (1940) hypothesis, as the value of cotton production rose during the period under investigation, the number of lynchings tended to decrease, and as the value of cotton production fell, the number of lynchings tended to rise. In chapter 15 we'll show you how to produce a scatterplot of these data. This is generally a good idea when studying correlations.

5.3 PARTIAL CORRELATION

Although Hovland and Sears (1940) analysed their results by computing a simple product-moment correlation, this method of data analysis would nowadays be considered inadequate on its own, because both variables are time series. The cotton production and lynching variables are measurements taken at consecutive points in time, and this means that the correlation could be *spurious*, not indicating the effects of cotton production values on lynchings as the researchers hypothesized, but merely the independent effect of time on each variable.

Any correlation between two variables may be due to the first having a causal effect on the second, the second having a causal effect on the first, or – a possibility often overlooked – a third variable having an independent causal effect on each of the others. A notorious example of this relates to the small but significant correlation between amount of television violence viewed and aggressive behaviour. This correlation *may* be due to television violence viewing causing aggressive behaviour, but another possibility is that a third factor, such as the personality trait of sensation-seeking, causes people both to view television violence and to behave aggressively, without any direct causal link between television violence viewing and aggressive behaviour.

In the case of the Hovland and Sears (1940) study that we discussed in section 5.2, it is possible that the negative correlation between the value of cotton production and the number of lynchings may be due to a third variable, in this case the dates of the measurements. A glance at Table 5.1 reveals that throughout most of the period that they studied, the value of cotton production tended to rise, perhaps because farming methods improved or simply because of inflation. It also appears that the number of lynchings tended to fall, at least from 1894 onwards, perhaps because racial prejudice declined or law enforcement improved. In other words, the correlation that Hovland and Sears reported might be due to the fact that both variables were time series that were tending to change in opposite directions, for quite independent reasons, during the period covered by the data.

To investigate this possibility, we're going to calculate a partial correlation coefficient. Partial correlations are used to investigate the linear relationship between two variables while controlling for or suppressing the effects of a third extraneous variable. Mathematically, values of the extraneous variable are, in effect, subtracted from each of the other two variables. In this case, we want to examine the relationship between the value of cotton production and the annual number of lynchings after removing the effects of time on both variables. Strictly speaking, this is a first-order partial correlation, because the effects of just one extraneous variable are controlled. If we controlled for two extraneous variables instead of just one, then it would be a second-order partial, and so on, and in this terminology an ordinary correlation coefficient is a zero-order partial. The underlying logic and mathematics of partial correlations are closely related to multiple regression, which we'll come to in chapter 12.

◆ First, make sure the data set **lynch.sav** is still in the Data Editor. Name a new variable in the **Variable View** that you can reach via the tab at the bottom-left of the Data Editor, insert a new row at the top, above **cotton**, and name it **date**. (If you've forgotten how to insert a new row, revise section 2.4.).

◆ Click the **Data View** tab to return to the data entry window and enter the dates from Table 5.1 into the first column.

◆ Save the input data for future reference by following the procedure described in section 2.7. If you haven't already saved these data in the previous section, so that it already has the right name, call the file **lynch.sav**.

◆ Click **Analyze** in the menu bar near the top of the SPSS Data Editor, and select **Correlate** in the drop-down menu that appears, exactly as you did before.
◆ Click **Partial...** in the submenu to get partial correlations.

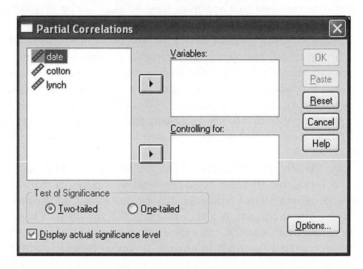

◆ The three variables in the left-hand source box are **date**, **cotton**, and **lynch**. Move **cotton** and **lynch** to the **Variables** box on the right, and move **date** to the **Controlling for:** box immediately below it.
◆ In the same dialog box, select the test of significance to be applied to the correlation coefficient. Once again, **Two-tailed** is the default, but you could choose **One-tailed** if you wished by clicking its radio button. Make sure that **Display actual significance level** is selected – put a tick in the check box if there isn't one there already.
◆ The dialog box has a button labelled **Options...**, and if you clicked it, a subdialog box would open in which you could request for means, standard deviations, and zero-order correlations to be displayed. We don't need any of the special options for this analysis.
◆ Click the **OK** button, and the Output Viewer will appear, displaying the partial correlation results.
◆ If you want to print a hard copy of the output, follow the procedure described in section 3.2.

Correlations

Control Variables			cotton	lynch
date	cotton	Correlation	1.000	-.212
		Significance (2-tailed)	.	.148
		df	0	46
	lynch	Correlation	-.212	1.000
		Significance (2-tailed)	.148	.
		df	46	0

As you can see, the partial correlation between the value of cotton production and the number of lynchings is still negative after controlling for date, but it is no longer significant and should therefore be attributed to chance. In a journal article or research monograph, we might report this as follows: "The partial correlation between the annual number of lynchings in the southern United States from 1882 to 1930 and the value of cotton production in the corresponding years, after controlling for date, is $r(46) = -.21$, *ns*, providing no significant evidence in support the causal hypothesis suggested by Hovland and Sears (1940)." An alternative way to report the correlation results is "$r = -.21$, $n = 46$, *ns* (two-tailed)". This provides a salutary lesson about correlations in general – whenever we find a correlation between two variables, we should always be alert to the possibility that there is a third extraneous variable that explains it.

5.4 SPEARMAN'S RHO

For convenience, let's calculate Spearman's rho from the data already entered in section 5.2, although the scores are measured on interval scales and we now know that the correlation is spurious.

◆ First, get back to the Data Editor by clicking **lynch – SPSS Data Editor** in the bar near the bottom of the Output Viewer.
◆ Click **Analyze** in the menu bar. Select **Correlate** in the drop-down menu, and then click **Bivariate...** in the submenu that appears. The Bivariate Correlations dialog box, which we've already shown you, will open again.
◆ Make sure that the two variables named **cotton** and **lynch** are in the right-hand box, which is labelled **Variables** – if necessary, select them and click the black arrow button to get them into the right-hand box (if you're unsure, review section 4.2).
◆ In the same dialog box, select the type of correlation coefficient you want, in this case **Spearman**. Make sure also that **Pearson** and **Kendall's tau-b** are deselected: if there are ticks in their check boxes, click the boxes to remove the ticks. Select which test of significance you want to be applied to your correlation. **Two-tailed** is the default, but you could have chosen **One-tailed,** if you wished, by clicking its radio button. To cause correlation coefficients significant at the 0.05 and 0.01 levels to be flagged with a single and a double asterisk, respectively, keep the tick in the check box beside **Flag significant correlations**.
◆ If you clicked the **Options...** button, you would open a sub-dialog box in which you could instruct SPSS to calculate means, standard deviations, cross-product deviations, and covariances, should you require them, and if you had some missing values, you could select a method of dealing with them. The system default for handling missing values is, as before, to exclude cases pairwise.
◆ When you are satisfied that everything in the Bivariate Correlations dialog box is as you want it to be, click the **OK** button, and the Output Viewer will reappear, displaying the results. If some of the results scroll off the window, use the scroll bars as explained in section 2.5.

◆ To print a hard copy of the output, follow the procedure described in section 3.2. You can select part of the data to print by first clicking or clicking and shift-clicking in the panel on the left, or by hiding part of the data via the minus/plus boxes, or double-clicking on the book symbols, beside their labels in the left-hand panel.

➔ Nonparametric Correlations

Correlations

			cotton	lynch
Spearman's rho	cotton	Correlation Coefficient	1.000	-.637**
		Sig. (2-tailed)	.	.000
		N	49	49
	lynch	Correlation Coefficient	-.637**	1.000
		Sig. (2-tailed)	.000	.
		N	49	49

**. Correlation is significant at the 0.01 level (2-tailed).

The output, headed **Nonparametric Correlations**, is presented in a matrix similar to the one for Pearson's correlation coefficient. The names of the two variables, namely **cotton** and **lynch**, are displayed, together with the value of Spearman's rho (another name for Spearman's rank correlation coefficient), $r_s = -.637$, the significance level ($p < .000$), and the number of cases ($N = 49$). Once again, the significance level of .000 should be interpreted as $p < .001$. If we were reporting these results, we'd write something like: "A large negative correlation was found between the annual number of lynchings that took place in the southern United States from 1882 to 1930 and the value of cotton production in the corresponding years, $r_s(47) = -.64$, $p < .001$ (two-tailed)." These results agree well with Pearson's product-moment correlation coefficient calculation in section 5.2, and this is to be expected.

◆ If you want to go straight on to the next chapter, click **File** in the menu bar near the top of the Output Viewer, then select **New** and click **Data**. If you want to exit from SPSS, click **File** in the menu bar, and then **Exit** at the bottom of the drop-down menu. If a dialog box appears asking you whether you want to save the contents of the Output Viewer, click **Yes** or **No**, and if **Yes**, follow the procedure in section 2.7. If you haven't already saved the input data, then a dialog will open asking you whether you want to save the contents of the Data Editor, and you should click **Yes** and save the data under the file name **lynch.sav**.

6 Chi-square Tests

6.1 BACKGROUND

The chi-square statistic is often symbolized by χ^2, the square of *chi*, the 22nd letter of the Greek alphabet. One use of the chi-square test is to determine whether or not two variables measured on nominal or categorical scales – in other words, variables that consist of frequencies or counts – are associated with each other. When it is used for that purpose it is called the chi-square test of association, or the chi-square test of independence. Another use is to determine the goodness of fit of a single variable measured on a nominal or categorical scale to a theoretical distribution. This is called the chi-square goodness-of-fit test, or the chi-square one-sample test. In either case, the test provides a means of determining whether a set of observed frequencies deviate significantly from a set of expected frequencies. The usual formula for calculating the statistic, called the Pearson chi-square test, is $\chi^2 = \Sigma(O - E)^2/E$, where O represents an observed frequency, E an expected frequency under the null hypothesis, and the summation is over all pairs of observed and expected frequencies.

For the chi-square test to be valid, the scores must consist of a random sample of data measured on nominal scales, or data from other types of scales reclassified into mutually exclusive categories so that they represent counts or frequencies. The scores must be independent of one another so that, for example, it is not usually permissible for scores in different categories to come from the same respondent or research subject. When the data are displayed in a contingency table larger than 2 × 2, none of the expected frequencies in the cells should be less than 1 and no more than 20 per cent should be less than 5. You will be warned by SPSS through a message in the output if these last assumptions are violated. For 2 × 2 contingency tables with small expected frequencies, SPSS uses Fisher's exact probability test, which does not require large expected frequencies in order to be valid.

6.2 THE CHI-SQUARE TEST OF ASSOCIATION

The results of a study of 554 people in Los Angeles who tried to give up cigarette smoking by themselves were reported in an article by Cohen et al. (1989). The researchers compared light smokers who smoked 20 or fewer cigarettes (one packet or less) per day with heavy smokers who smoked more than 20 cigarettes per day. After 12 months, the numbers of participants who were still abstaining and the numbers who had relapsed were as shown in the following contingency table of observed frequencies:

	Abstaining	Relapsed
Light smokers	45	285
Heavy smokers	14	210

The researchers analysed these data by using the chi-square test of association, and you are going to check their results. It is clear that 45 of the 330 light smokers

(13 per cent) were still abstaining after 12 months, whereas only 14 of the 224 heavy smokers (6 per cent) were still abstaining after 12 months. But is this difference statistically significant? Note that we could have asked the same question the other way round: 45 of the 59 abstainers (76 per cent) were light smokers, whereas only 285 of the 495 relapsers (58 per cent) were light smokers, but is this difference significant? Whichever way the question is asked, it amounts to the same thing: Is there a significant association in these results between light versus heavy smoking on the one hand and continuing abstinence versus relapse after 12 months on the other?

This is one of the cases we warned you about at the beginning of section 2.3 in which the data must be entered in a single column of the Data Editor, with grouping variables in separate columns to show (in this case) whether each score refers to light or heavy smokers and whether it refers to abstaining or relapsed smokers. You can't enter the scores as they are set out in the table above; instead you should enter them as shown in Table 6.1.

Table 6.1 Smoking data input format

Smoking	Status	Count
1	1	45
1	2	285
2	1	14
2	2	210

The first column is a grouping variable showing whether the scores refer to participants who were light (1) or heavy (2) smokers at the start of the study. The second column is a grouping variable showing whether the scores refer to participants whose status at the 12-month follow-up was abstaining (1) or relapsed (2). We could just as well have used the value label of 2 for light smokers and 1 for heavy smokers, or 2 for those who remained abstinent and 1 for those who relapsed, or we could have used other numbers: the choice of values for a grouping variable is arbitrary and does not affect the results of the analysis. The third column, of course, contains the actual scores – the frequency counts shown in the earlier table. This table is merely another way of displaying the same data using grouping variables. Now let us show you how to prepare for data input.

6.3 NAMING VARIABLES AND LABELLING VALUES

First, the variables must be named and the values of the grouping variables properly labelled.

◆ If you've just restarted SPSS and you see the "What would you like to do?" dialog box, then click the radio button beside **Type in data**, followed by **OK**.

◆ Make sure that the Data Editor is empty, then click the **Variable View** tab at the bottom of the Data Editor, and in the first three rows of the **Name** column type **smoking** for the first variable, **status** for the second, and **count** for the third. (If you've forgotten how to name variables, then read section 2.3 again.)

◆ Now define the value labels 1 and 2 of the **smoking** variable. To do this, move the mouse pointer along the **smoking** variable row and click inside the cell headed **Values**. Then click the grey button that appears on the right-hand side of the cell, and the Value Labels dialog box will open.

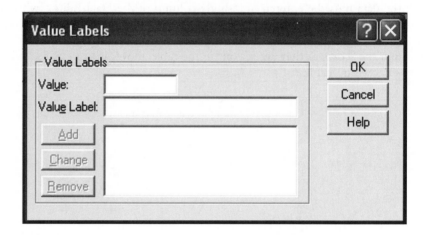

◆ Inside the text box labelled **Value**, type the numeral **1**. Click inside the text box labelled **Value Label** and type **light**. Click the **Add** button. The value label **1.00 = "light"** will appear in the list box below. Repeat the process to define the value 2: in the text box labelled **Value**, type the numeral **2**, then click in the text box labelled **Value Label** and type **heavy** and click **Add**. The value label **2.00 = "heavy"** will be added to the list box. Click the button labelled **OK**.

◆ Repeat the process to define the value labels of the **status** variable. Move the mouse pointer along the **status** variable row and click inside the cell under the **Values** heading. Then click the grey button on the right-hand side of the cell to open the Value Labels dialog box again.

◆ In the text box labelled **Value**, type the numeral **1**. Click in the text box labelled **Value Label** and type **abstain**. Click the **Add** button. Repeat the process to define the value 2: in the text box labelled **Value**, type the numeral **2**, then click in the text box labelled **Value Label** and type **relapse** and click **Add**. At this point, in SPSS 16 only, there is the ability to run a spelling check on the labels, if you feel you need to check them, by clicking the **spelling** button. Finally, in this box, click **OK**. The numbers that you enter here are the codes that you are assigning to represent different groups of participants or answers that the particip- ants have given you. This process of giving numbers to responses is called coding. Typically, things like gender are coded as 1 = male, 2 = female. It is also useful to know that you can copy and paste the attributes of one variable to another variable, which saves you time. If, for example, you wanted to type in a 1 to 7 scale with labels for 100 different questions, you could type in the values and labels for the first variable and then select that label box, copy it, select the other variable's labels boxes, and paste it into them.

♦ Because the third variable, **count**, is not a grouping variable, you don't have to define value labels for it – its values are the actual scores. But you do have to tell SPSS that this variable contains frequency scores. The way you do it is rather strange, and you'd never guess it without being told. An official *SPSS for Windows Base System User's Guide* (Norušis, 1993) doesn't even mention it in its section on the chi-square test (pp. 389–392), and people often get stuck at this point. Click **Data** in the menu bar near the top of the Data Editor, and choose the command **Weight Cases...** at the bottom of the drop-down menu. The Weight Cases dialog box will open.

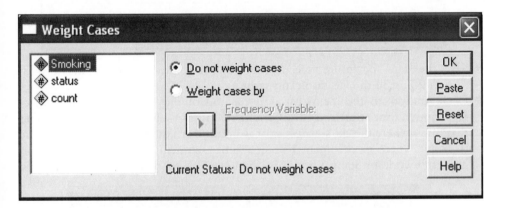

♦ Click the radio button labelled **Weight cases by**. Click the variable name **count** on the left, and then click the black arrow button to move it into the list box labelled **Frequency Variable**. Click **OK**. Click the **Data View** tab (now activated) at the bottom of the window to get back to the data input window of the Data Editor with the variables properly labelled.

6.4 DATA INPUT AND ANALYSIS

You are now ready to key in the data and initiate the computation.

♦ Key in the data in the format shown in Table 6.1, following the procedure described in section 2.4. Note that in the Data Editor you can either see the full variable labels or the numbers that you typed in to represent them, and you can toggle between the two using the little icon at the top that looks like a luggage label. (We show both versions in the screenshot, so that you can see what we mean.)

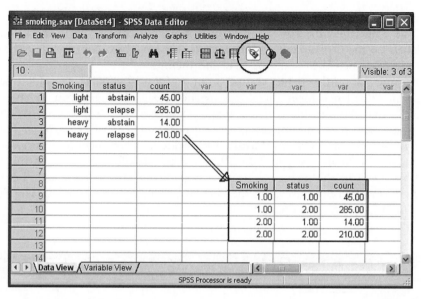

- ◆ Save the data for future reference by following the procedure described in section 2.7. Call the file **smoking.sav**.
- ◆ Click **Analyze** in the menu bar near the top of the Data Editor, then select **Descriptive Statistics**) and click **Crosstabs...** in the submenu. Try to remember that this is where the chi-square test of association is hidden. People often struggle to find it. There's a chi-square test on another submenu that's easier to find, but it doesn't work for doing a test of association. We'll show it to you in section 6.5.

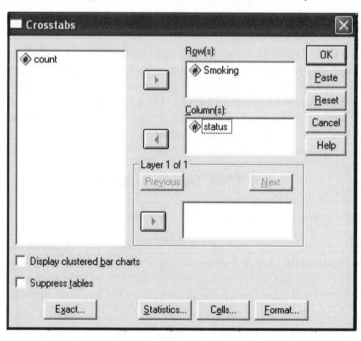

◆ The Crosstabs dialog box will open. Click the variable name **smoking**, if it isn't already highlighted, and move it to the box labelled **R̲ow(s)** by clicking the black arrow button. This tells SPSS that the row variable is **smoking**. Now click **status** and move it to the box labelled **C̲olumn(s)**. Leave **count** where it is. You have already told SPSS that this is the frequency variable.

◆ Elsewhere in the Crosstabs dialog box, click the button labelled **S̲tatistics...**, and a sub-dialog box entitled Crosstabs: Statistics will open. Select **Chi̲-square** by clicking the check box beside it so that a tick appears in the box. At this point you could also choose various other statistics suitable for nominal data: the contingency coefficient, phi coefficient, Cramér's *V*, or (Goodman–Kruskal) lambda, which are all chi-square-based measures of association for categorical data, or the uncertainty coefficient, which is a measure of how much information about one variable is provided by the other, and various nonparametric correlations and other procedures are also available. In the Statistics dialog box, click **Continue**.

◆ When you are returned to the Crosstabs dialog box, click **C̲ells...**, and a new sub-dialog box called Crosstabs: Cell Display will open. Here you can customize the output to suit your needs. To display both observed and expected frequencies, which will make interpretation of the results easier, ensure that both **O̲bserved** and **E̲xpected** are selected by clicking in the check boxes beside them so that ticks appear there. Remember (see section 6.1) that there are constraints on the expected frequencies that are acceptable for chi-square tests. You could also, if you wished, select percentages (row, column, and total), which would display within each cell the percentage of the cell frequency relative to the row, column and/or total frequency, which are often useful in interpreting the output if you can imagine percentages better than frequencies. You could also select residuals (unstandardized, standardized, and adjusted standardized), which would display differences between observed and expected frequencies. You don't have to select any of these to get the row and column totals of the contingency table itself; these will be displayed anyway. Click **Continue**, and when you are returned to the Crosstabs dialog box, click **OK**.

◆ The Output Viewer will appear with the results of the chi-square analysis displayed. If some of the results scroll off the window, use the scroll bars as explained in section 2.5.

◆ To print a hard copy of the output, click **F̲ile** in the menu bar near the top of the window, followed by **P̲rint...**, and follow the procedure described in section 3.2. If you want to print just one of the tables, click its name in the left-hand panel, or click the table itself, and then click **P̲rint...** and then click the **S̲election** radio button in the Print dialog box.

Crosstabs

Case Processing Summary

	Cases					
	Valid		Missing		Total	
	N	Percent	N	Percent	N	Percent
Smoking * status	554	100.0%	0	.0%	554	100.0%

Smoking * status Crosstabulation

			status		
			abstain	relapse	Total
Smoking	light	Count	45	285	330
		Expected Count	35.1	294.9	330.0
	heavy	Count	14	210	224
		Expected Count	23.9	200.1	224.0
Total		Count	59	495	554
		Expected Count	59.0	495.0	554.0

Chi-Square Tests

	Value	df	Asymp. Sig. (2-sided)	Exact Sig. (2-sided)	Exact Sig. (1-sided)
Pearson Chi-Square	7.650[b]	1	.006		
Continuity Correction[a]	6.894	1	.009		
Likelihood Ratio	8.136	1	.004		
Fisher's Exact Test				.007	.004
Linear-by-Linear Association	7.636	1	.006		
N of Valid Cases	554				

a. Computed only for a 2x2 table

b. 0 cells (.0%) have expected count less than 5. The minimum expected count is 23.86.

The output includes, first, a summary of the input data, showing that there were no missing data in this case. Second, there is a contingency table showing both the observed frequencies (the input data) and the expected frequencies (based on an assumption of no association between the two variables), together with the row and column totals (often called marginals). This second table is properly labelled with the variable names and value labels that you assigned. The third table includes among other things the following information: the values of both Pearson's chi-square and the likelihood ratio chi-square test, the corresponding degrees of freedom and asymptotic (approximated) two-tailed significance levels, and (because this was a 2×2 analysis) the two-tailed and one-tailed significance levels calculated from Fisher's exact probability test. Also shown in this third table, labelled Continuity Correction, is the chi-square value, degrees of freedom, and two-tailed significance level for Pearson's chi-square test with a (Yates) correction for continuity, which some statisticians recommend for use with 2×2 contingency tables.

The value of Pearson's chi-square, with one degree of freedom, is shown to be 7.650, with a two-tailed significance level of $p = .006$. Note that the significance level is the probability of obtaining a chi-square at least as large as this on the basis of chance alone; that is, under the null hypothesis that there is no association. The smaller the significance level, the less probable this is, and by convention, results of significance tests are usually considered significant, and the null hypothesis is rejected, if p is smaller than .05, so that the probability of obtaining results as extreme as the results actually obtained is less than 5 per cent, or 1 in 20. In the article from which the data were taken (Cohen et al., 1989), Pearson's chi-square was reported as $\chi^2(1) = 7.65$, $p < .01$ (two-tailed), and these results agree perfectly with ours. The two variables are significantly associated with each other. The authors concluded that "heavy smoking self-quitters are less successful at long-term quitting than their light smoking counterparts" (p. 1363).

Sometimes, the data that you want to analyse with a chi-square test are not in a summary form as shown in Table 6.1, but instead are in a raw form in a large data set. For example, there may be two columns, the first showing whether each participant is a light or heavy smoker and the second column showing whether each one was still abstaining or had relapsed. Data like that, with all 554 participant observations listed in full, can be analysed with a chi-square test, without the need to put the data into a summary table first. To do it, you would click **Analyze**, then **Descriptive Statistics**, then **Crosstabs....** Instead of having three variables, and needing to specify the frequency variable with "weight cases", you would instead have only two variables. You would put one variable into the **Row(s)** box and the other into the **Column(s)** box, then click **Statistics...** and put a tick in the check box next to **Chi-square**. Click **Continue** to leave the submenu, then **OK** in the Crosstabs dialog box to run the test. There is no need to do the "weight cases" step in this situation. The output statistics would be the same as those produced from the summary data above.

6.5 THE CHI-SQUARE GOODNESS-OF-FIT TEST

When a chi-square test is used to compare an observed frequency distribution with a distribution that is expected on theoretical grounds, it is called a chi-square goodness-of-fit test or a chi-square one-sample test. Mathematically, the method of computing it is essentially the same as for a chi-square test of association, but the expected frequencies are supplied by the analyst rather than being estimated from the observed frequencies, and the procedure for performing the analysis in SPSS is quite different.

Feller (1968, pp. 160–161) discussed an intriguing example arising from the bombing of London during the Second World War. An area of south London was hit by over 500 bombs, and most residents believed that the bombs were not falling randomly but were clustering in certain small areas. So strong was this belief that many people abandoned their homes after their neighbourhoods had been hit by bombs. If south London is divided into 576 sectors or neighbourhoods of just one square kilometre each, then the numbers of sectors that experienced zero, one, two, three, four, and five or more hits are shown in Table 6.2, together with the theoretical numbers of sectors that would be expected to experience the corresponding numbers of hits according to the Poisson probability distribution if the bombs fell completely at random.

The observed and expected distributions look remarkably similar, which suggests that the belief of wartime Londoners that the bombs clustered in certain neighbourhoods was merely an illusion or a superstition. To establish objectively whether the

Table 6.2 Bombs falling on London

Number of hits	0	1	2	3	4	5+
Sectors observed	229	211	93	35	7	1
Sectors expected	227	211	98	31	7	2

two distributions are significantly different, you should perform a chi-square goodness-of-fit test by carrying out the following steps:

◆ Close the Output Viewer by clicking **File** in the menu bar near the top of the Viewer, followed by **Close**. A dialog box will appear asking you whether you want to save the data that are currently in the Output Viewer. Click **No**. You will be returned to the Data Editor.

◆ If you still have data from the previous analysis in the Data Editor, click **File** in the menu bar near the top of the Data Editor, select **New** in the menu that drops down, and click **Data** in the submenu that appears. If you haven't saved the data currently in the Data Editor, a dialog box will appear asking you whether you want to save them, in which case you should click **Yes** and then follow the procedure described in section 2.7 to save the file under the file name **smoking.sav**; otherwise, click **No**.

◆ Following the same procedure as in section 6.3, click the **Variable View** tab at the bottom of the window, and rename the first variable of the Data Editor **hits** and the second **count**. Then label the **hits** variable as follows so that the lowest value, namely 0, represents zero hits, 1 represents 1 hit, and so on. In the text box labelled **Value** type **0** and in the **Value Label** text box type **0 hits**, then type **1** and **1 hit**, **2** and **2 hits**, **3** and **3 hits**, **4** and **4 hits**, and finally **5** and **5+ hits**. Click **OK**.

◆ Tell SPSS which variable contains the frequency scores. Click **Data** in the menu bar near the top of the Data Editor, and choose the command **Weight Cases...** at the bottom of the drop-down menu. In the Weight Cases dialog box that opens, click the radio button beside **Weight cases by**. Click the variable name **count**, if it isn't already highlighted, and then click the black arrow button to move it into the list box labelled **Frequency Variable**. Click **OK**.

◆ Click the **Data View** tab at the bottom of the window to get back to the data input window of the Data Editor. Enter the data in the following format:

hits	count
0	229
1	211
2	93
3	35
4	7
5	1

◆ Unless you've reconfigured your variables in the Data View window, these will appear in the Data Editor with two decimal places (0.00 instead of 0, 229.00 instead of 229, and so on), but it does not affect the calculations. If you want to get rid of the two decimal places, then go to the Variable View window and click inside the cell in the Decimals column for the variable that you want, then type the number of decimal places required; for example, type **0**. Save the input data for future reference by following the procedure described in section 2.7. Call the file **bombs.sav**.

◆ Click **Analyze** in the menu bar near the top of the Data Editor, then select **Nonparametric Tests** and click **Chi-Square...** in the submenu. The Chi-Square Test dialog box will open.

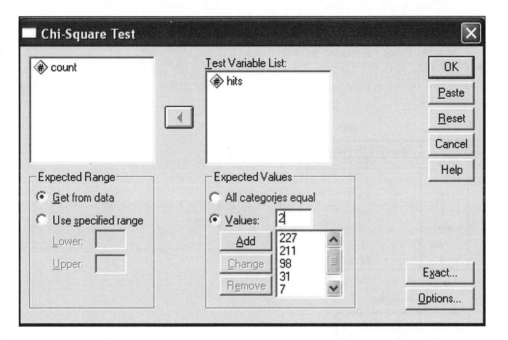

◆ Select the categorical variable **hits** on the left by clicking it, and transfer it to the **Test Variable List** on the right by clicking the black arrow button.

◆ If the expected frequencies were all equal, you could at this stage use the default **All categories equal**. But in this case the expected frequencies vary from one category to another, and you haven't entered them yet. Click the radio button labelled **Values** and type the expected frequency for category 0, namely **227**, into the text box beside it. Click the **Add** button, which will have lit up. Now type in the expected frequency for category 1, namely **211**, click the **Add** button, and continue in the same way with the rest of the expected frequencies in order from Table 6.2. SPSS assumes that the first expected frequency that you enter is associated with the first value of the categorical variable, the second with the second value, and so on. The expected frequencies will appear in that order in the list box below.

◆ In the same Chi-Square Test dialog box there is also an **Options...** button that opens a sub-dialog box where you could ask for descriptive statistics (mean, minimum, maximum, standard deviation, number of cases, and quartile values of the distribution), and where you could determine how missing values were handled if you had any.

◆ Notice also the part of the Chi-Square Test dialog box labelled **Expected Range**. The radio button **Get from data** is lit up by default, and it is usually satisfactory, unless you want the analysis to be performed across only some (rather than all) of the categories of the test variable (**hits**). But if the observed count had been zero in one of the categories of the test variable, then the analysis would fail. For example, it would fail if the frequency for 5+ hits were zero instead of 1. But you could get round this problem by clicking the **Use specified range** radio button and then typing in the lower and upper bound of the range of the test variable, namely 0 and 5 in this hypothetical example. But you don't have any zero observed scores, so there's no need for this.

◆ Click **OK**, and the Output Viewer will appear with the results of the analysis. If some of the results scroll off the window, use the scroll bars as explained in section 2.5.

hits

	Observed N	Expected N	Residual
0 hits	229	227.0	2.0
1 hit	211	211.0	.0
2 hits	93	98.0	-5.0
3 hits	35	31.0	4.0
4 hits	7	7.0	.0
5+ hits	1	2.0	-1.0
Total	576		

Test Statistics

	hits
Chi-Square [a]	1.289
df	5
Asymp. Sig.	.936

a. 1 cells (16.7%) have expected frequencies less than 5. The minimum expected cell frequency is 2.0.

◆ To print a hard copy of the output, follow the procedure described in section 3.2. To print onvly a selection of the output, first select the desired table by clicking its name in the left-hand panel of the Output Viewer or by clicking the table itself, then use the procedure described in section 3.3.

The output is quite straightforward and easy to understand. First there is a table labelled **hits** showing the observed and expected frequencies. The first column lists the categories of the test variable using the value labels that you attached to them, the second shows the observed number of hits in each category, the third shows the expected number of hits in each category, and the fourth shows the residuals for each category – the difference between observed and expected frequencies in each category. If the bombs had fallen nonrandomly, then the residuals would have been largest in the categories with either many hits or no hits and smallest in the middle categories. The second table, labelled **Test Statistics**, shows the results of the chi-square goodness-of-fit test. It shows the value of chi-square to be 1.289, the degrees of freedom (df) 5, and the asymptotic or approximated significance (Asymp. Sig.) .936. (Arguably, there should be one less degree of freedom, because one was used for the parameter needed to calculate the Poisson frequencies, but that's a complex statistical question, and life is short.)

The results could be reported something like this: "The observed frequencies do not differ significantly from the expected frequencies, based on the Poisson probability distribution: $\chi^2(5) = 1.29$, $p = .94$." What this implies is that if the bombs really did fall at random, and if the bombing were to be repeated many times, then the deviation from the theoretical random distribution would be at least as great in about 94 per cent of cases. In other words, the observed frequencies were remarkably close to those expected by chance, in spite of what Londoners thought at the time – the apparent clustering was an illusion.

◆ Close the Output Viewer by clicking **File** in the menu bar near the top of the window, followed by **Close**. When a dialog box appears asking you whether you want to save the contents of the Output Viewer, click **Yes** or **No**, and if **Yes**, follow the procedure in section 2.7. You will be returned to the Data Editor.

◆ If you want to go straight on to the next chapter, click **File** in the menu bar near the top of the Data Editor, select **New**, then click **Data** in the submenu. If you want to exit from SPSS, then click **File** in the menu bar followed by **Exit** (see section 2.8). In either case, if you have not saved the input data and a dialog box appears asking you whether you want to save the contents of the Data Editor, click **Yes** and save it under the file name **bombs.sav**.

7 Independent-samples, Paired-samples, and One-sample *t* Tests

7.1 BACKGROUND

In this chapter we'll describe two versions of a test that is most often used to establish the significance of a difference between the means of two samples of scores. It is calculated by dividing the difference between the means by the standard error of this difference. Its full name is Student's t test, not because students often use it, though they do, but because "Student" was the pen name of the English statistician William Sealy Gosset, who developed the theory behind it in 1908 while working for the Guinness brewery in Dublin, before the test was refined by another English statistician called Karl Pearson. Guinness employees were not allowed to publish their research findings, but a special concession was granted to Gosset to publish his work under a pen name.

The independent-samples t test, which we'll describe in section 7.2, is used to test for a significant difference between the means of two independent or unrelated samples of scores. The paired-samples or related-groups or matched-groups t test, described in section 7.3, is used when the two samples of scores are correlated, usually because they represent either pairs of repeated measures from the same individuals or scores from two matched groups. Whenever the paired-samples t test is appropriate, the numbers of scores in the two groups must be equal, because each score in one group is paired with a score in the other, but the independent-samples t test can be used with groups of unequal size. In section 7.4 we'll explain the one-sample t test, which is used to determine whether the mean of a single sample of scores differs significantly from some specified value.

The t test assumes that the scores are measured on at least an interval scale, that they are normally distributed, and (for the standard independent-samples and paired-samples tests) that the variances in the two groups are approximately equal. Many statisticians nowadays consider the t test to be fairly robust against moderate violations of the second and third assumptions, which are called the normality and homogeneity of variance assumptions, at least when equal-sized groups are being compared. But if the scores are measured on only an ordinal scale, or if their distributions are markedly nonnormal or their variances markedly unequal, then the equivalent nonparametric tests described in chapter 8, which are only slightly less powerful than the t test, are sometimes preferred.

7.2 THE INDEPENDENT-SAMPLES t TEST

An experiment was reported by Fazio et al. (1995) in which an unobtrusive (disguised) measure of racial attitudes was applied to 45 white and 8 black students in the United States. The students, working at computer terminals, were shown a series of 24 words, half of which were positive in meaning (e.g., *attractive, likeable, wonderful*) and half negative (e.g., *annoying, disgusting, offensive*), and they were asked to decide as quickly as possible, by pressing a key labelled *good* or a key labelled *bad*, to which category each word belonged. Each word was preceded by a photograph of a white or a black person. It was assumed that for people with strongly negative attitudes towards black people, a black face immediately preceding a positive word would cause interference and slow down their responses. The researchers computed an estimate of each student's attitude towards black people by comparing the effects of black and white faces on response times to the positive and negative words. The scores, on a scale in which negative scores indicate negative attitudes and positive scores positive attitudes towards black people, were as follows:

White students: −9, −8, −7, −6, −6, −6, −6, −5, −5, −5, −5, −4, −4, −4, −4, −4, −4, −4, −3, −3, −3, −3, −3, −3, −2, −2, −2, −2, −2, −2, −2, −1, −1, −1, −1, −1, 0, 0, 0, 0, 0, 1, 2, 2, 2
Black students: 0, 1, 1, 2, 2, 3, 6, 7

The scores of the white students look generally lower than those of the black students, but are they *significantly* lower, or could the difference be attributed to chance, especially with such a small sample of black students? An objective answer to this question will be provided by the results of an independent-samples *t* test.

◆ If you've just restarted SPSS and you see the "What would you like to do?" dialog box, then click the radio button beside **Type in data**, followed by **OK**.
◆ Your first task, as always, is to define your variables. For this analysis, you're going to put all the scores into a single column of the Data Editor, with a grouping variable in another column indicating which group each score belongs to. So you should begin by clicking the **Variable View** tab at the bottom of the Data Editor. In the first two rows of the **Name** column, name the first variable **group** and the second **attitude**. If you've forgotten how to name variables, review section 2.3.
◆ Next, type in labels for the values of the **group** variable so that **1** stands for **white** and **2** stands for **black**. If you've forgotten how to do this, review section 6.3. The **attitude** variable is not a grouping variable, so you don't have to define value labels for it – its values are the actual scores. Click the **Data View** tab at the bottom of the Data Editor to get back to the data input window with both variables properly labelled.
◆ Now key the data into the Data Editor. If you've forgotten how to key in data, review section 2.4. Key the values of the grouping variable into the first column: type the numeral **1** in the first 45 rows and the numeral **2** in the next eight rows. Then key the attitude scores in the second column, starting with the 45 scores of the white students and ending with the 8 scores of the black students.
◆ Save the data for future reference by following the procedure described in section 2.7. Call the file **fazio.sav**.
◆ Click **Analyze** in the menu bar near the top of the Data Editor, then select **Compare Means**.

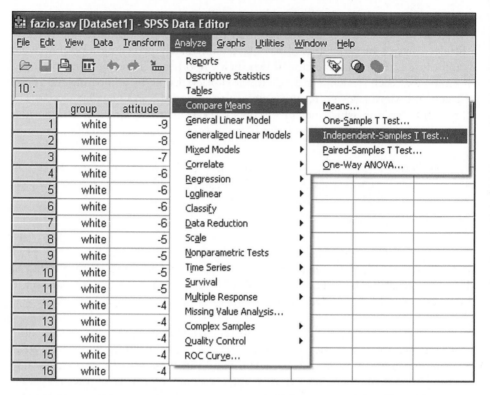

◆ In the **Compare Means** submenu, click **Independent-Samples T Test...**, and the Independent-Samples T Test dialog box will open.

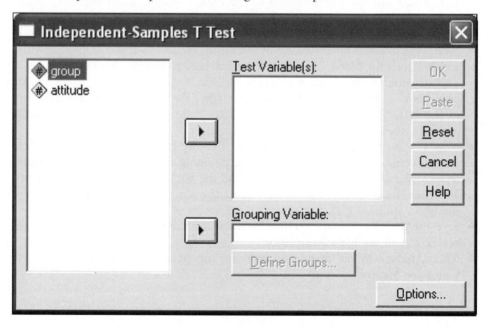

◆ You need to move the variable name **attitude** on the left to the box labelled **Test Variable(s),** and the variable **group** to the box labelled **Grouping Variable**. Select **attitude** by clicking it, and transfer it to the **Test Variable(s)** box on the right by clicking the upper arrow button. Click **group** on the left, and transfer it to the **Grouping Variable** box with the lower arrow button.

◆ When the variable **group** reappears in the **Grouping Variable** box, it will have acquired a pair of question marks in brackets after its name: **group[? ?]**. The question marks indicate ignorance and concern on the part of SPSS as to which groups the labels **1** and **2** refer to. Click **Define Groups...,** now lit up, and the Define Groups sub-dialog box will open.

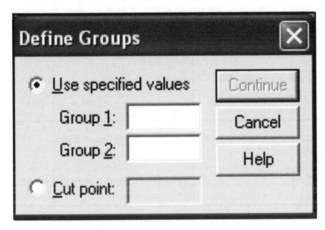

◆ In the text box marked **Group 1** type **1**, then click in the text box marked **Group 2** and type **2**. Only numerical values can be entered in these text boxes: they are values of the grouping variable used to classify the data in the Data Editor. If you had used different numbers to label the two groups in the Data Editor, then you would have had to enter those numbers here. Click **Continue**, which will have lit up.

◆ You will find yourself back in the Independent-Samples T Test dialog box. There is a button marked **Options...,** which opens a sub-dialog box where you could change the confidence interval that will be supplied with the output (the system default is the usual 95 per cent confidence interval). In this sub-dialog box you could also determine how SPSS deals with missing data, if you had any. The system default is to exclude missing data analysis-by-analysis if you perform several *t* tests, in other words to use all the available data for each separate analysis. For the vast majority of *t* tests, you wouldn't want to alter these defaults.

◆ In the Independent-Samples T Test dialog box, click **OK**, and the results of the analysis will be displayed in the Output Viewer. If some of the data scroll off the window, then use the scroll bars to view them (see section 2.5).

◆ To print a hard copy of the output, follow the procedure described in section 3.2. To print a selection, first click or shift-click the desired names in the panel on the left, or click the tables themselves, then use the procedure described in section 3.3.

T-Test

Group Statistics

	group	N	Mean	Std. Deviation	Std. Error Mean
attitude	white	45	-2.8000	2.59895	.38743
	black	8	2.7500	2.49285	.88135

Independent Samples Test

		Levene's Test for Equality of Variances		t-test for Equality of Means					95% Confidence Interval of the Difference	
		F	Sig.	t	df	Sig. (2-tailed)	Mean Difference	Std. Error Difference	Lower	Upper
attitude	Equal variances assumed	.061	.806	-5.596	51	.000	-5.5500	.9917	-7.5410	-3.5590
	Equal variances not assumed			-5.765	9.908	.000	-5.5500	.9627	-7.6978	-3.4022

The output is not difficult to understand. The first table provides some descriptive statistics for the variable labelled ATTITUDE: the number of cases, mean, standard deviation (Std. Deviation), and standard error of the mean (Std. Error Mean) for the white and black groups separately. The second table provides the *t* test results, first, in the top row, with the assumption of equal variances (homogeneity of variance), using a pooled variance estimate, and below that without the assumption of equal variances, using separate variance estimates. The results of Levene's test for equality of variances are given to help you decide whether the assumption of equal variances holds. As you can see, the Levene's test result is nonsignificant ($F = .061$, $p = .806$), which indicates that the variances of the two groups are not significantly different, so the homogeneity of variance assumption wasn't violated.

With equal variances assumed, $t = -5.596$ (the minus sign is immaterial, reflecting merely the order of the two means in the numerator of the formula used to calculate *t*, so its value may be given as 5.596 or 5.60), the degrees of freedom (df) are 51, and the two-tailed significance level is .000, which does not mean that it is exactly zero but merely that it is less than .001. The second line of the second table gives the same results using separate variance estimates, which you would report if the variances been markedly different, if there had been a significant Levene's test result of $p < .05$. Lastly, the final part of the table shows, for both types of analysis, the mean difference (−5.5500), the standard error of the difference, and the lower and upper 95 per cent confidence bounds of the difference. The mean difference is the size of the gap between the two means, in this case the difference between −2.80 and 2.75. This can be useful if you look at it in relation to the standard deviations or want to compute Cohen's *d* by hand.

Looking at the means in the first table, it is clear that, even on the unobtrusive or disguised measure of attitudes towards black people used in this research, black students showed significantly more positive attitudes than white students. The results of the analysis are usually written as follows, "An independent-samples *t* test showed that black students' attitudes to black faces ($M = 2.75$, $SD = 2.49$) were significantly more positive than the white students' attitudes to black faces ($M = -2.80$, $SD = 2.60$), $t(51) = 5.60$, $p < .001$ (two-tailed)." The means are significantly different and cannot be attributed to chance, as the obtained *p* value is less than the critical value of .05. If you're not sure how to interpret *p* values, review our explanation in section 6.4.

◆ Click **File** in the menu bar near the top of the Output Viewer, followed by **Close**. When a dialog box opens asking you whether you want to save the contents of the Output Viewer, click **Yes** or **No**, and if **Yes**, follow the procedure in section 2.7. You will be returned to the Data Editor.
◆ Click **File** in the menu bar near the top of the Data Editor, select **New**, and click **Data** in the submenu. If you have not already saved the input data, then when a dialog box opens asking whether you wish to save the contents of the Data Editor, click **Yes** so that you don't have to key the scores in again when we re-analyse them in section 8.2. We suggested that you name the file **fazio.sav**. If you've forgotten how to save data, review section 2.7.

7.3 THE PAIRED-SAMPLES *T* TEST

Knox, Morgan, and Hilgard (1974) reported an experiment in which eight university students who had been selected for high hypnotic susceptibility were exposed to pain in hypnosis under two conditions: with suggestions from the hypnotist designed to induce anaesthesia, and without any anaesthesia suggestions. The order of the treatment conditions with and without anaesthesia was counterbalanced – half the students took part in the session without anaesthesia on one day and the session with anaesthesia on the following day, and the other half experienced the anaesthesia and no-anaesthesia conditions in the reverse order. Pain was induced by the method of ischaemia. A tourniquet was applied to each student's arm just above the elbow to obstruct the flow of blood, and the student was instructed to squeeze a hand-exercising device in a controlled manner for 80 seconds and then to relax. When ischaemic pain is induced in this way without hypnosis, the pain begins to mount as soon as the person stops exercising and becomes extremely intense after about eight minutes. In the experiment, the students rated the intensity of the pain on a scale in which zero indicated "no pain sensation", 10 "a very strong sensation of pain", and numbers above 10 even more intense pain sensations. The students' ratings at eight minutes of ischaemia were as shown in Table 7.1.

Table 7.1 Hypnotic anaesthesia

Participant	No anaesthesia	Anaesthesia
1	5	1
2	11	0
3	18	0
4	11	2
5	9	2
6	9	2
7	5	1
8	11.5	0

The ratings of pain without hypnotic anaesthesia look higher than those with hypnotic anaesthesia, but is the difference statistically significant, or could it be attributed to chance in such a small sample? You can discover the answer with the paired-samples *t* test as follows:

◆ If the input data from the previous analysis are still in the Data Editor, then click **File** in the menu bar near the top of the window, select **New**, and click **Data** in the submenu. If you haven't saved the previous data, save them under the file name **fazio.sav** when prompted.
◆ Name the two variables that will go in the first two columns of the Data Editor. Click the **Variable View** tab at the bottom of the Data Editor and follow the procedure described in section 2.3. In the **Name** column, name the first variable **nohypan** and the second **hypan**. Neither is a grouping variable, so there's no need to define value labels.
◆ Get back to the data input window by clicking the **Data View** tab at the bottom of the Data Editor, and key the data into the first two columns (if you've forgotten how to do this, see section 2.4). Put scores from the no hypnotic anaesthesia condition in the **nohypan** column and scores from the hypnotic anaesthesia condition in the **hypan** column.
◆ Save the data for future reference by following the procedure described in section 2.7. Call the file **knox.sav**.
◆ Click **Analyze** in the menu bar near the top of the Data Editor, then select **Compare Means**.

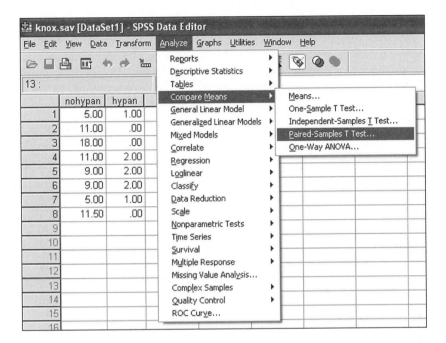

◆ In the submenu that drops down, click **Paired-Samples T Test...**, and the Paired-Samples T Test dialog box will open.

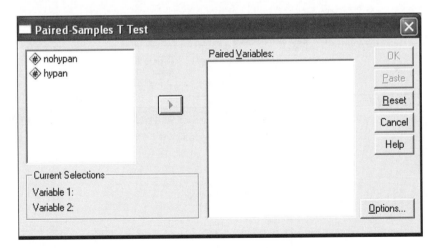

◆ You must move both variables on the left to the **Paired Variables** box on the right. Click the variable names **nohypan** and **hypan**, so that they appear in the Current Selections list at the bottom as **Variable 1: nohypan** and **Variable 2: hypan**, respectively. Then click the black arrow button and the pair of variables will leap together into the **Paired Variables** box.

◆ There is a button marked **Options...** that opens a sub-dialog box in which you could alter the confidence interval for the difference between the means from the usual default of 95 per cent. In the same dialog box you could also determine the treatment of missing values – the system default is to exclude missing data analysis by analysis if you perform several *t* tests; in other words to use all available data for each separate analysis. For the vast majority of *t* tests, you would not need to alter these defaults.

◆ In the Paired-Samples T Test dialog box, click **OK**, and the results of the analysis will be displayed in the Output Viewer.

◆ To print a hard copy of the output, follow the procedure described in section 3.2. To print only a selection of the output, first click or shift-click the corresponding names in the panel on the left, or click the tables themselves, then use the procedure described in section 3.3. Before printing, you may see by using print preview that a table such as a *t* test is too wide to print on just one page. If you are happy for the table to break across pages then leave it, but if you want it to shrink to fit on to one page then there is a way. First double-click the too-wide table to open it, then either right-click any part of the table or go to **Format,** and then click **Table Properties....** In the Table Properties dialog box click the tab labelled **Printing**, and then click to put a tick in the box next to **Rescale wide table to fit page**. Similarly, if you had a table that was too long for the page you could make it fit by ticking the **Rescale long table to fit page** box. Next click **OK** and then close the table. When you next check Print Preview or print the document, the table will have shrunk to fit.

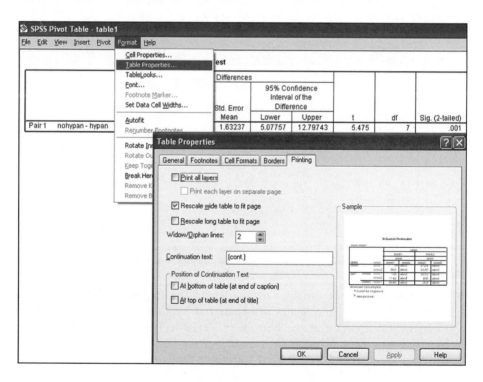

While we're talking about the output, it's worth pointing out that in SPSS you can add colour to your output if you want to highlight certain cells, by double-clicking on the table to open it and then either right-clicking on any part of the table or going to **Format** and then **Cell Properties...**. Next go to the tab labelled **Shading** (or, in SPSS 16, **Font and Background**) and change the background colour to the colour you want. Finally, close the properties box by clicking **OK** and then close the table, and your colour will appear.

T-Test

Paired Samples Statistics

		Mean	N	Std. Deviation	Std. Error Mean
Pair 1	nohypan	9.9375	8	4.14417	1.46518
	hypan	1.0000	8	.92582	.32733

Paired Samples Correlations

		N	Correlation	Sig.
Pair 1	nohypan & hypan	8	-.428	.290

Paired Samples Test

		Paired Differences							
					95% Confidence Interval of the Difference				
		Mean	Std. Deviation	Std. Error Mean	Lower	Upper	t	df	Sig. (2-tailed)
Pair 1	nohypan - hypan	8.9375	4.6170	1.6324	5.0776	12.7974	5.475	7	.001

The first table provides some descriptive statistics. For the NOHYPAN (no hypnotic anaesthesia) and HYPAN (hypnotic anaesthesia) groups separately, it shows the mean, number of scores (N), standard deviation, and standard error of the mean. The second table shows the number of pairs (N), the correlation between the two groups, and the significance of the correlation (Sig.). The third table shows the mean, standard deviation, standard error of the mean, and 95 per cent confidence interval of the paired difference, the value of *t*, the degrees of freedom (df), and the two-tailed significance level.

The value of *t* is shown to be 5.475, with degrees of freedom 7 and two-tailed significance level .001. If you're not sure how to interpret significance levels, then review our explanation in section 6.4. The results would usually be reported along the lines of "A paired-samples *t* test showed that the perceived intensity of pain was significantly higher in the No Hypnotic Anaesthesia condition ($M = 9.94$, $SD = 4.14$) than in the Hypnotic Anaesthesia condition ($M = 1.00$, $SD = 0.93$), $t(7) = 5.48$, *p* < .001 (two-tailed)." These figures agree exactly with those given in the original article by Knox, Morgan, and Hilgard (1974), who concluded, in part, that "for highly hypnotizable subjects, suggested anaesthesia is successful, leading in some cases to the complete elimination of pain and suffering, and averaging, in this experiment, pain and suffering reduction of about 90%" (p. 846).

◆ Click **File** in the file menu near the top of the Output Viewer, then **Close**. When a dialog box appears asking whether you want to save the contents of the Output Viewer, click **Yes** or **No**, and if **Yes**, follow the procedure in section 2.7. You will be returned to the Data Editor.

◆ If you haven't saved the current input data, then save them now (see section 2.7) so that you don't have to key the scores in again when we re-analyse them in section 8.3. We suggested that you call the file **knox.sav**. Keep the data in the Data Editor for now; we'll reuse them in the one-sample *t* test that follows.

7.4 THE ONE-SAMPLE *T* TEST

This *t* test is occasionally used to determine the significance of the difference between the mean of a sample of scores and some specified value. This test can be used, for example, to determine whether the mean of a sample of IQ scores is significantly different from 100, which is average by definition. To save time and trouble we'll illustrate the technique with data from the previous section (7.3). Suppose that you want to determine whether the mean of the students' pain ratings under hypnotic anaesthesia was significantly different from zero.

◆ If the data from the hypnosis experiment are no longer in the Data Editor, then load the **knox.sav** file. Click **File** in the menu bar near the top of the Data Editor, select **Open**, click **Data** in the submenu, then follow the procedure described in section 3.1. If you neglected to save the data, then key them in again (see section 2.4).

◆ Click **Analyze** in the menu bar near the top of the Data Editor, select **Compare Means**, click **One-Sample T Test...** in the submenu, and the One-Sample T Test dialog box will open.

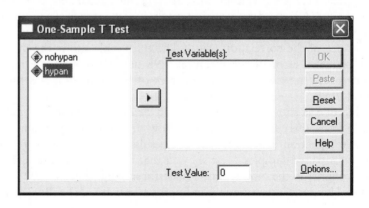

◆ Select the variable **hypan** (the hypnotic group of scores) on the left by clicking it, and transfer it to the box labelled **Test Variable(s)** by clicking the black arrow button.
◆ Make sure that the **Test Value** text box below is showing zero. If you were comparing the mean with some value other than zero, then you would have to type the specified value into the text box.
◆ There is an **Options...** button that opens the familiar sub-dialog box in which you could, if you wished, alter the confidence interval to be displayed in the output. You could also change the method of handling missing data, if you had any, from the default of excluding missing values analysis by analysis, that is, using all the available scores for each test.
◆ Click **OK**, and the results will appear in the Output Viewer.

T-Test

One-Sample Statistics

	N	Mean	Std. Deviation	Std. Error Mean
hypan	8	1.0000	.92582	.32733

One-Sample Test

	Test Value = 0					
					95% Confidence Interval of the Difference	
	t	df	Sig. (2-tailed)	Mean Difference	Lower	Upper
hypan	3.055	7	.018	1.00000	.2260	1.7740

The first table shows the number of scores (8), the mean (1.0000), the standard deviation (.92582), and the standard error of the mean (.32733). The second table shows that the value of t is 3.055, the degrees of freedom (df) 7, the two-tailed significance .018, the mean difference from the specified value 1.0000, and the lower and upper 95 per cent confidence bounds of the difference .2260 and 1.7740, respectively. The results are usually presented as "$t(7) = 3.06$, $p < .02$ (two-tailed)". (If you're not sure how to interpret p values, review our explanation in section 6.4.) They show that the hypnotically anaesthetized subjects in the experiment reported by Knox, Morgan, and Hilgard (1974) gave pain ratings that were significantly different from (higher than) zero.

◆ Click **File** in the file menu near the top of the Output Viewer, then **Close**. When a dialog box appears asking whether you want to save the contents of the Output Viewer, click **Yes** or **No**, and if **Yes**, follow the procedure in section 2.7. You will be returned to the Data Editor.

◆ If you want to go straight on to the next chapter, click **File** in the menu bar, select **New**, then click **Data** in the submenu. If you want to exit from SPSS at this point, click **File** in the menu bar near the top of the Output Viewer, and then **Exit** at the bottom of the menu that drops down. In either case, if for any reason you haven't saved the input data, then click **Yes** and save them under the file name `knox.sav` when you are prompted.

8 Mann–Whitney *U* and Wilcoxon Matched-pairs Tests

8.1 BACKGROUND

The tests described in this chapter are nonparametric or distribution-free equivalents of the *t* tests described in chapter 7. The Mann–Whitney *U* test, which we'll describe in section 8.2, is a nonparametric equivalent of the independent-samples *t* test, and the Wilcoxon matched-pairs test, which we'll describe in section 8.3, is a nonparametric equivalent of the paired-samples *t* test. They can be used to test the significance of differences between samples of scores that represent at least ordinal measurement. The Mann–Whitney *U* test, named after the Austrian-born US mathematician Henry Berthold Mann and the US statistician Donald Ransom Whitney, who published the test in 1947, involves combining the scores from the two groups, ranking them, and then calculating the statistic *U*, which is the number of times a score from the second group precedes a score from the first group in the ranking. The Wilcoxon matched-pairs test, also called the Wilcoxon signed-ranks test, named after the Irish statistician Frank Wilcoxon, who developed the test in 1945, involves first calculating the absolute values of the differences between the two variables for each individual or case and then ranking these differences from smallest to largest, and the test statistic *T* is computed from the sums of ranks for negative and positive differences.

8.2 THE MANN–WHITNEY *U* TEST

To save time, you are going to re-analyse the data from Fazio et al. (1995) that you used in section 7.2. We suggested that you save the data under the file name **fazio.sav**.

◆ If you've just restarted SPSS and the "What would you like to do?" dialog box has opened in front of the Data Editor, then click the radio button beside **Open an existing data source**, then click **OK**, and open **fazio.sav** using the procedure described in section 3.1.
◆ If there is no dialog box, then load the file by clicking **File** in the menu bar near the top of the Data Editor, selecting **Open**, clicking **Data** in the submenu, and open **fazio.sav** following the procedure described in section 3.1. If you didn't save the file, key the data in again and name the variables as described towards the beginning of section 7.2.
◆ Click **Analyze** in the menu bar near the top of the Data Editor and select **Nonparametric Tests**.

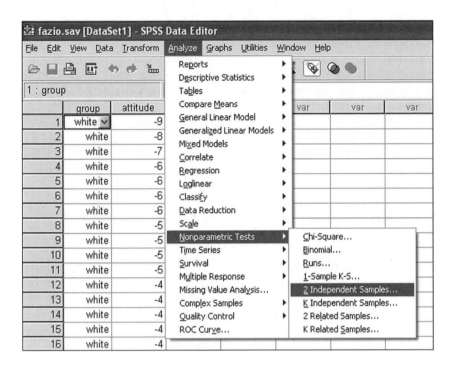

◆ Click **2 Independent Samples...** in the submenu to open the Two-Independent-Samples Tests dialog box.

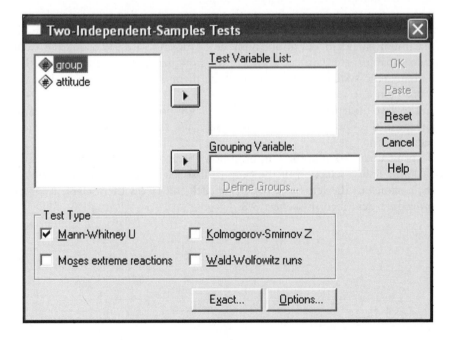

◆ You need to move the variable **attitude** on the left to the box labelled **T̲est Variable List** and the variable labelled **group** to the box labelled **G̲rouping Variable**. Select **attitude** by clicking it to highlight it, and transfer it to the **T̲est Variable List** box on the right by clicking the upper arrow button. Click **group** on the left, and transfer it to the **Grouping Variable** box by clicking the lower arrow button.

◆ When the variable **group** reappears in the **Grouping Variable** box, it will have acquired a pair of question marks in brackets after its name: **group[? ?]**. You need to tell SPSS which groups the labels **1** and **2** refer to. Click **D̲efine Groups...** and a sub-dialog box similar to one we showed you in section 7.2 will open.

◆ In the Define Groups sub-dialog box, find the text box marked **Group 1̲** and type **1**, then click in the text box marked **Group 2̲** and type **2**. Only numerical values can be entered in these boxes: they are values of the grouping variable used to classify the data in the Data Editor. Click **Continue**.

◆ Back in the Two-Independent-Samples Tests dialog box, from the group labelled **Test Type**, choose **M̲ann-Whitney U** by clicking in the check box beside its name so that a tick appears there, if it isn't there already. Make sure that **K̲olmogorov-Smirnov Z**, **Mo̲ses extreme reactions**, and **W̲ald-Wolfowitz runs** are all deselected (to remove a tick, just click it). These are alternative nonparametric tests that can be performed on two independent samples of scores.

◆ The dialog box has a button labelled **E̲xact...** that opens the Exact Tests sub-dialog box in which you could instruct SPSS to perform an exact randomization test, a Monte Carlo simulation based on repeated random samples of the data, or an asymptotic test based on the distribution of the test statistic. This last method is the default (and most usual) procedure.

◆ There is also an **O̲ptions...** button that opens a sub-dialog box in which you could ask for descriptive statistics to be supplied with the output (the mean, minimum, maximum, standard deviation, number of missing cases, and quartile values for each variable), and you could determine how missing values are handled, if you had any (the system default is to exclude them on a test-by-test basis if you run more than one test).

◆ In the Two-Independent-Samples Tests dialog box, click **OK**, and the results will appear in the Output Viewer. If necessary, use the scroll bars to view them (see section 2.5).

◆ To print a hard copy of the output, follow the procedure described in section 3.2. To print only a selection of the output, first select the desired tables by clicking their names in the left-hand panel, or click the tables themselves, then use the procedure described in section 3.3.

NPar Tests

Mann-Whitney Test

Ranks

	group	N	Mean Rank	Sum of Ranks
attitude	white	45	23.37	1051.50
	black	8	47.44	379.50
	Total	53		

Test Statistics[b]

	attitude
Mann-Whitney U	16.500
Wilcoxon W	1051.500
Z	-4.082
Asymp. Sig. (2-tailed)	.000
Exact Sig. [2*(1-tailed Sig.)]	.000[a]

a. Not corrected for ties.

b. Grouping Variable: group

The first table shows the mean rank and sum of ranks of the 45 white and 8 black participants. The second gives the value of the Mann–Whitney U statistic (16.500) together with the asymptotic (approximated) and exact two-tailed significance levels (both .000, to be interpreted as less than .001). Also included in the second table is the value of the statistic Wilcoxon W (the sum of ranks for the first group) and of Z (the standardized normal approximation of the test statistic, from which the asymptotic significance level is estimated). The usual style for reporting the results is simply "$U(51) = 16.50$, $p < .001$, two-tailed". (If you're not sure how to interpret p values, review our explanation in section 6.4.) These results agree well with those of section 7.2, which is to be expected, because when the Mann–Whitney U test is applied to data that are suitable for the independent-samples t test, its power-efficiency is about 95 per cent, even for moderate-sized samples, and approaches 95.5 as sample sizes increase.

◆ Click **File** in the file menu near the top of the Output Viewer, then **Close**. When a dialog box appears asking whether you want to save the contents of the Output Viewer, click **Yes** or **No**, and if **Yes**, follow the procedure in section 2.7. You will be returned to the Data Editor.
◆ Click **File** in the menu bar near the top of the Data Editor, select **New**, then click **Data** in the submenu. If you haven't already saved the data from the Fazio

experiment, you may save them by clicking **Yes** when a dialog box opens asking whether you wish to save the contents of the Data Editor. Use the file name `fazio.sav`.

8.3 THE WILCOXON MATCHED-PAIRS TEST

Now you are going to re-analyse the data from Knox, Morgan, and Hilgard (1974), discussed in section 7.3, which we advised you to save under the file name **knox.sav**. If you have the file, then load it up by clicking **File** in the menu bar near the top of the Data Editor, selecting **Open**, clicking **Data** in the submenu, and following the procedure described in section 3.1. If you don't have a copy of the data, key the scores in again and name the variables as described towards the beginning of section 7.3.

◆ Click **Analyze** in the menu bar near the top of the Data Editor, select **Non-parametric Tests**, then click **2 Related Samples...** in the submenu, and the Two-Related-Samples Tests dialog box will open.

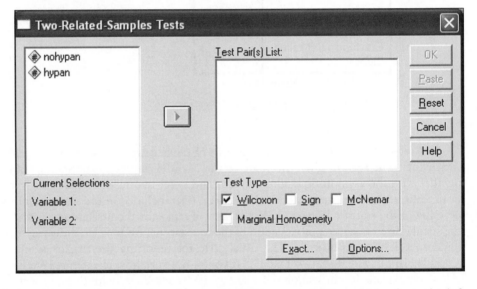

◆ As with the paired-samples *t* test, you need to move both variables from the left to the **Test Pair(s) List** on the right. Click the variable names **nohypan** and **hypan**, so that they appear in the **Current Selections** list at the bottom as **Variable 1: nohypan** and **Variable 2: hypan**, respectively. Then click the black arrow button and the pair of variables will leap together into the **Test Pair(s) List**. If you're running SPSS 16, there is no **Current Selections** list; instead, you need to select each variable in turn, and press the arrow each time, to move it to the **Test Pairs:** box.

◆ In the **Test Type** group, choose **Wilcoxon** by clicking in the check box beside its name so that a tick appears there, if it isn't there already. Make sure that **Sign**, **McNemar**, and **Marginal Homogeneity** are all deselected (to remove a tick, just click it). These are alternative nonparametric tests that can be performed on two related samples of scores.

◆ Once again, there is an **Exact...** button that opens the Exact Tests sub-dialog box in which you could instruct SPSS to perform an exact randomization test, a Monte Carlo simulation based on repeated random samples of the data, or an asymptotic test based on the distribution of the test statistic, the last method being the default and usual procedure.

◆ There is also an **Options...** button that opens a sub-dialog box in which you could ask for descriptive statistics to be supplied with the output (the mean, minimum, maximum, standard deviation, number of missing cases, and quartile values for each variable), and you could determine how missing values are handled, if you had any (the system default is to exclude them on a test-by-test basis if you run more than one test).

◆ In the Two-Related-Samples Tests dialog box, click **OK**, and the results of the analysis will appear in the Output Viewer.

◆ To print a hard copy of the output, follow the procedure described in section 3.2. To print only a selection of the output, first click the corresponding label in the panel on the left, or click the table itself, then use the procedure described in section 3.3.

➡ NPar Tests

Wilcoxon Signed Ranks Test

Ranks

		N	Mean Rank	Sum of Ranks
hypan - nohypan	Negative Ranks	8[a]	4.50	36.00
	Positive Ranks	0[b]	.00	.00
	Ties	0[c]		
	Total	8		

a. hypan < nohypan

b. hypan > nohypan

c. hypan = nohypan

Test Statistics[b]

	hypan - nohypan
Z	-2.527[a]
Asymp. Sig. (2-tailed)	.012

a. Based on positive ranks.

b. Wilcoxon Signed Ranks Test

The first table shows the number of negative ranks (the number of times the rank of variable 1 is less than the rank of variable 2), the number of positive ranks (the number of times the rank of variable 1 is greater than the rank of variable 2), and the number of ties (scores with the same rank). The notes below the table make the directions of the differences clear. In this experiment, the ranks of scores in the hypnotic anaesthesia group were lower than those in the no hypnotic anaesthesia group in all eight cases, with no ties. The second table shows the value of Z, the standardized normal approximation to the test statistic and the asymptotic two-tailed significance estimated from the normal approximation. The minus sign attached to Z is unimportant, reflecting merely the order in which the groups were compared. Values of Z are associated with exactly the same probability whether they are positive or negative, because the standardized normal distribution is symmetrical about a mean of zero. The results of this analysis would normally be reported as follows: "$Z = 2.53$, $p = .01$, two-tailed". The results agree well with those of the paired-samples t test of section 7.3, although at a slightly lower significance level. When the Wilcoxon test is applied to data that are suitable for the paired-samples t test, its power-efficiency is about 95 per cent for small samples.

◆ Click **File** in the file menu near the top of the Output Viewer, then **Close**. When a dialog box appears asking whether you want to save the contents of the Output Viewer, click **Yes** or **No**, and if **Yes**, follow the procedure in section 2.7. You will be returned to the Data Editor.

◆ If you want to go straight on to the next chapter, click **File** in the menu bar, select **New**, then click **Data** in the submenu. Otherwise, exit from SPSS by clicking **File** in the menu bar near the top of the Output Viewer, and then **Exit** at the bottom of the menu that drops down. If you have not already saved the input data, you may wish to save them under the file name **knox.sav** when prompted.

9 One-way Analysis of Variance

9.1 BACKGROUND

One-way analysis of variance (one-way ANOVA) is a statistical procedure for test-ing the significance of the differences among several independent group means by partitioning the total variance in the dependent variable into effects due to different levels of the independent variable, which in ANOVA is sometimes called the factor, plus error variance. You may find it helpful to think of one-way analysis of variance as a generalization of the independent-samples t test designed to determine the signi-ficance of the differences among three or more (rather than just two) group means. Or to put it another way, the independent-samples t test is merely a special case of one-way analysis of variance for determining the significance of the difference between means when there are just two means to compare. You could, in fact, use one-way ANOVA to get the identical result.

The analysis described in this chapter is based on the assumption that the scores are all statistically independent of one another. If the scores are not independent, usually because they come from repeated measures on the same group of individuals, then the analysis requires a slightly different procedure, which we'll describe in chapter 11.

9.2 DATA INPUT

Corston and Colman (1996) reported the results of an experiment in which female students attempted to use a mouse pointer to track a small square as it moved erratically around a computer screen. The women who participated in the experiment were randomly assigned to three treatment conditions in which they performed the task either alone, in the presence of a female audience, or in the presence of a male audience. The percentages of time on target in the three audience conditions were as shown in Table 9.1.

The tracking scores look distinctly higher in the Female audience condition than in the Alone and Male audience conditions, but are the means of the three audience conditions significantly different from one another? Did the manipulation of the independent variable have a significant effect on the tracking scores? One-way ANOVA will answer these questions.

First, the data must be entered into the Data Editor in a single column, with a grouping variable in a separate column to indicate to which group each score belongs. We introduced you to this method of formatting data, which is necessary for many SPSS analyses, in sections 6.2 and 6.3. To enter the audience effect data, proceed as follows.

◆ If you've just restarted SPSS and the "What would you like to do?" dialog box has opened, then click the radio button beside **Type in data**, followed by **OK**.
◆ Name the two variables that will be typed into the first two columns of the Data Editor. Click the **Variable View** tab at the bottom of the window and follow the procedure described in section 2.3 if you've forgotten. In the **Name** column, name the first variable **audience** and the second **score**.

Table 9.1   Audience effects

Participant	Alone	Female	Male
		Audience condition	
1	31.4	41.0	16.2
2	2.8	46.0	21.8
3	34.8	54.0	26.8
4	27.0	36.4	23.2
5	9.8	50.4	40.8
6	24.4	31.0	12.0
7	18.4	47.2	13.6
8	14.2	51.4	16.0
9	21.0	45.8	35.2
10	20.2	40.0	22.2
11	12.2	45.8	25.4
12	12.2	25.8	2.8

◆ The first variable, **audience**, is a grouping variable, so you have to define labels for the values of this variable. If you've forgotten how to do this, review section 6.3. Insert value labels so that **1** stands for **alone** and **2** stands for **female**, and **3** stands for **male**. The **score** variable is not a grouping variable and does not need any value labels assigned to it – its values are the scores themselves. Click the **Data View** tab at the bottom of the Data Editor to get back to the data input window with both variables properly labelled.

◆ Back in the data input window of the Data Editor, key all the data from the table above into the first two columns of the Data Editor. The scores should be entered in the first 36 rows of the second column and the grouping variable in the first column as follows (we show just a few rows):

	audience	score
1	1.00	31.40
2	1.00	2.80
3	1.00	34.80
4	1.00	27.00
5	1.00	9.80
6	1.00	24.40

13	2.00	41.00
14	2.00	46.00
15	2.00	54.00
16	2.00	36.40
17	2.00	50.40
18	2.00	31.00

◆ Save the data for future reference by following the procedure described in section 2.7. Call the file **audience.sav**.

9.3 ANALYSIS

The analysis of one-way ANOVA data is quite straightforward.

◆ Click **Analyze** near the top of the Data Editor and select **Compare Means**.

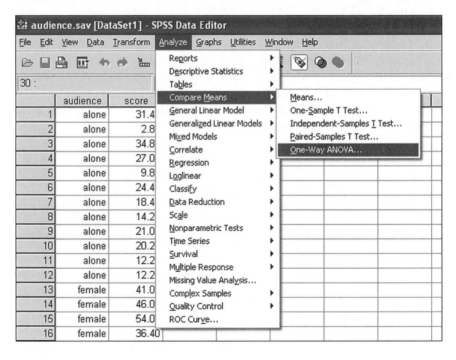

◆ Click **One-Way ANOVA...** in the submenu, and the One-Way ANOVA dialog box will open.

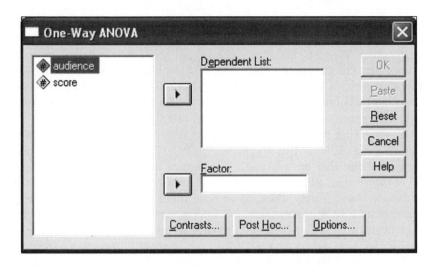

♦ You need to move the variable **score** to the **Dependent List** box and **audience** to the **Factor** box. Click **score** on the left, then click the upper arrow button pointing to the box labelled **Dependent List** on the right. Then click **audience** on the left, followed by the lower arrow button pointing to the box labelled **Factor**.

♦ If you wished to calculate contrasts – planned *t* test comparisons of pairs of means – you could at this stage click **Contrasts...** and a sub-dialog box would open. This should not be used for post hoc or a posteriori multiple comparisons (see immediately below).

♦ Click **Post Hoc...** and the Post Hoc Multiple Comparisons sub-dialog box will open.

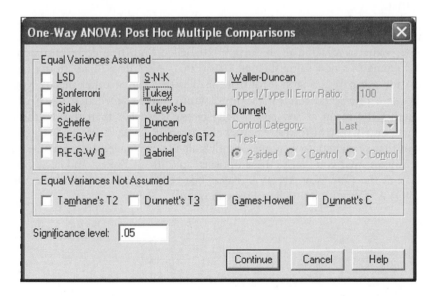

◆ You have a choice of no fewer than 18 different methods of making post hoc or a posteriori multiple comparisons between the means. These tests show which means differ from which others if the overall result reveals that there is *some* difference between the three means. The first test listed is **LSD**, the least-significant difference test. It uses pairwise *t* tests to compare each mean with every other mean but does not make any adjustment for the fact that several comparisons are made using the same data and therefore offers no protection against a Type I error – rejecting the null hypothesis of no effect when it is true. The probability that each *t* is significant by chance is .05, but if you perform several *t* tests, then the probability that *at least one* is significance by chance is actually higher than .05, because the test is repeated more than once – if you performed 100 *t* tests on purely random data, then about 5 of them would be significant at $p < .05$ purely by chance. **Bonferroni**, the Bonferroni *t* test, adjusts the significance level crudely and drastically: if three comparisons are made at $p < .05$, it requires a significance level of $.05/3 = .017$ for each separate comparison. The other tests in the group labelled **Equal Variances Assumed** are the most commonly used multiple comparison procedures, each with its own advantages and disadvantages, including **Scheffe** (the Scheffé test), **S-N-K** (the Student-Newman–Keuls test, also called the Newman–Keuls test), **Tukey** (Tukey's honestly significant difference test or the Tukey-HSD test), **Tukey's-b** (Tukey's b test), **Duncan** (Duncan's multiple range test), and **Dunnett** (Dunnett's specialized test for comparing a single control mean with a set of other means). There are further tests in the group labelled **Equal Variances Not Assumed**. We recommend Tukey's honestly significant difference test (the Tukey-HSD test) for most purposes, because it is widely used, and it offers adequate protection against a Type I error without being excessively conservative, as are the Bonferroni *t* test and Scheffé's test.

◆ Click the check box beside **Tukey** so that a tick appears there, and make sure that the other options are deselected by clicking in their check boxes if there are ticks in them.

◆ In the same Post Hoc Multiple Comparisons sub-dialog box, you could if you wished change the default significance level of the test from $p < .05$ to some other value by clicking in the text box labelled **Significance level**, deleting .05, and typing in a new value such as .01 or .001. Also, if you had chosen Dunnett's test for comparing a single control mean with a set of other means, you could choose a one-tailed test by clicking a radio button labelled **< Control** to test whether the mean at any level of the factor is smaller than that of the control mean, or **> Control** to test whether the mean at any level of the factor is greater than that of the control mean. The default is a two-tailed test. For the moment we suggest that you ignore these options, apart from **Tukey**, and click **Continue**.

◆ Back in the One-Way ANOVA dialog box, Click **Options...** and the One-Way ANOVA: Options sub-dialog box will open.

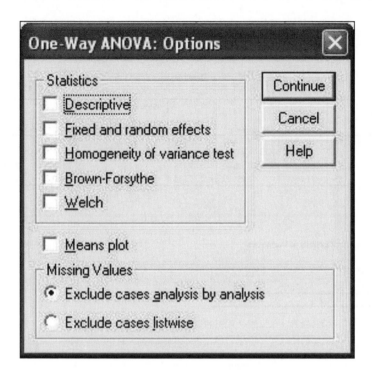

◆ The Statistics group allows you to ask for **Descriptive** statistics, which will cause SPSS to supply the number of cases, mean, standard deviation, standard error, minimum, maximum, and 95 per cent confidence interval of the dependent variable in each group. The means are almost always useful for interpreting the results, so click the check box beside **Descriptive** to put a tick there. Click the check box beside **Homogeneity of variance test** so that SPSS supplies the results of the Levene test, because it is an assumption of one-way ANOVA that the variances of the groups are approximately equal. If you wished, you could also click the check box beside **Means plot** to request a graph showing the means for each group on the dependent variable, and if you had any missing data you could use the radio button to change from the default method of handling missing values. Click **Continue**.

◆ Back in the One-Way ANOVA dialog box click **OK**, and the Output Viewer will appear with the results of the analysis.

◆ To print a hard copy of the output, follow the procedure described in section 3.2. To print only a selection of the output, first click the corresponding label in the panel on the left, or click the table itself, then use the procedure described in section 3.3.

9.4 RESULTS

Descriptives

score

	N	Mean	Std. Deviation	Std. Error	95% Confidence Interval for Mean		Minimum	Maximum
					Lower Bound	Upper Bound		
alone	12	19.0333	9.36602	2.70374	13.0824	24.9842	2.80	34.80
female	12	42.9000	8.44727	2.43852	37.5329	48.2671	25.80	54.00
male	12	21.3333	10.30140	2.97376	14.7881	27.8785	2.80	40.80
Total	36	27.7556	14.21999	2.37000	22.9442	32.5669	2.80	54.00

Test of Homogeneity of Variances

score

Levene Statistic	df1	df2	Sig.
.098	2	33	.907

ANOVA

score

	Sum of Squares	df	Mean Square	F	Sig.
Between Groups	4160.116	2	2080.058	23.530	.000
Within Groups	2917.173	33	88.399		
Total	7077.289	35			

Post Hoc Tests

Multiple Comparisons

Dependent Variable: score

Tukey HSD

(I) audience	(J) audience	Mean Difference (I-J)	Std. Error	Sig.	95% Confidence Interval	
					Lower Bound	Upper Bound
alone	female	-23.86667*	3.83838	.000	-33.2853	-14.4481
	male	-2.30000	3.83838	.821	-11.7186	7.1186
female	alone	23.86667*	3.83838	.000	14.4481	33.2853
	male	21.56667*	3.83838	.000	12.1481	30.9853
male	alone	2.30000	3.83838	.821	-7.1186	11.7186
	female	-21.56667*	3.83838	.000	-30.9853	-12.1481

*. The mean difference is significant at the .05 level.

Homogeneous Subsets

score

Tukey HSD[a]

| audience | N | Subset for alpha = .05 | |
		1	2
alone	12	19.0333	
male	12	21.3333	
female	12		42.9000
Sig.		.821	1.000

Means for groups in homogeneous subsets are displayed.

a. Uses Harmonic Mean Sample Size = 12.000.

The first table provides the descriptive statistics that you requested. For each of the three treatment conditions, Alone, Female, and Male, the table shows the number of scores, mean, standard deviation, standard error, lower and upper bounds of the 95 per cent confidence interval, minimum, and maximum, and in the bottom line, labelled Total, these statistics are all supplied for the combined groups. The most important data here are the three means. It is clear that the mean for the Female audience condition (42.9000) is higher than the other two means (19.0333 and 21.3333), but it is not yet clear whether these differences are significant.

The second table supplies the results of the Levene test of homogeneity of variance. The results are nonsignificant (the significance is far greater than .05), showing that there is no reason to believe that the variances of the three groups are different from one another, which would violate the homogeneity of variance assumption of ANOVA and make the results difficult to interpret.

The third table is a standard ANOVA table showing the sum of squares, degrees of freedom (df), and mean square or variance estimates for the between-groups variance and the within-groups variance, the value of F (the between-groups variance divided by the within-groups variance), and the significance (Sig.) of the F ratio. The results show that the three means are significantly different from one another: the significance level of the F ratio is given as .000 (which you should interpret as meaning that p is less than .001). All that the basic one-way ANOVA test establishes is that there is some significant difference among the three means. Multiple comparisons are needed to establish where the differences lie.

The fourth and fifth tables show the results of the Tukey-HSD multiple comparison test in slightly different ways. Both tables show the results of multiple pairwise comparisons among the three groups, representing the three audience conditions: Alone, Male audience, and Female audience. In the fourth table, the first pair of rows in the body of the table shows that the Alone group mean is significantly different from the Female group mean (an asterisk against the mean difference indicates a difference significant at the .05 level) but not from the Male group mean. The second pair of rows shows that the Female group mean is significantly different from the Alone group mean and also from the Male group mean. The third pair of rows shows that the Male group mean is not significantly different from the Alone group mean but is significantly different from the Female group mean. Various descriptive statistics are also listed in this table.

In the fifth and final table, the three groups are divided into what are called homogeneous subsets. The Alone and Male groups are in one homogeneous subset, and the Female group is in another. This means that the means of the Alone and Male groups are not significantly different from each other (in other words they form a homogeneous subset) according to the Tukey-HSD test, at the significance level chosen, but they are both significantly different from the mean of the Female group. As you can see in the same table, the means of the Alone and Male groups are 19.0333 and 21.3333, respectively. These means are quite close together, and they are both much smaller than the mean of the Female group, which is 42.9000.

We may therefore conclude, as Corston and Colman (1996) did, that the audience condition had a significant effect on the performance of women in the computer-based tracking task. The results of the ANOVA are normally written something like this: "Mean scores differed significantly across the three treatment conditions: $F(2, 33) = 23.53$, $p < .001$. Post hoc Tukey-HSD tests showed that, in terms of percentage of time on target, the women who performed the task in the presence of a female audience scored significantly higher ($M = 42.90$) than the women who performed the task either alone ($M = 19.03$) or in the presence of a male audience ($M = 21.33$), and that no other differences were statistically significant." (If you're not sure how to interpret p values, review our explanation in section 6.4.) SPSS does not have an option for calculating the effect size of the result for the one-way ANOVA, unless you carry out the one-way using the Univariate option of the General Linear Model for the analysis instead. It is easy enough, however, to calculate the effect size eta squared by hand using the following formula: eta squared = sum of squares between groups divided by total sum of squares. Both of these figures can be seen in the third ANOVA output table and in our example we would calculate that $\eta^2 = 4160.116/7077.289 = 0.588$, which is a very large effect.

◆ Click **File** in the file menu near the top of the Output Viewer, then **Close**. When a dialog box appears asking whether you want to save the contents of the Output Viewer, click **Yes** or **No**, and if **Yes**, follow the procedure in section 2.7. You will be returned to the Data Editor.

◆ If you want to continue with the next chapter now, click **File** in the menu bar, select **New**, then click **Data** in the submenu. Otherwise, exit from SPSS by clicking **File** in the menu bar near the top of the Output Viewer, and then **Exit** at the bottom of the menu that drops down. If you have not already saved the input data, a dialog box will open, and you may wish to save them under the file name **audience.sav**.

10 Multifactorial Analysis of Variance

10.1 BACKGROUND

Multifactorial analysis of variance (multifactorial ANOVA) is an extension of one-way ANOVA, which you covered in chapter 9. It is used for analysing the simultaneous effects of two or more independent variables, usually called factors, on a dependent variable. In multifactorial ANOVA, the differences among several group means are analysed by partitioning the total variance in the dependent variable into effects due to each of the factors, called main effects, interactions between the factors, and error variance.

The feature of multifactorial ANOVA that differentiates it from one-way ANOVA is the inclusion of interaction terms in the statistical model. The results of a factorial experiment – one involving two or more independent variables or factors – could, of course, be analysed by applying one-way ANOVA to each factor separately; but this approach is often considered to be an error, partly because it fails to take account of possible interaction effects. Imagine an experiment designed to examine the effects of age (younger versus older) and gender (female versus male) on the performance of children on a spatial reasoning task. Suppose the results showed no significant main effects; in other words, no significant difference between the mean scores of the boys and the girls and no significant difference between the mean scores of younger and older children. The interaction between the two factors, gender and age, could nevertheless be significant if, for example, in the younger age group girls outperformed boys (because girls tend to mature earlier than boys) whereas in the older age group boys outperformed girls (because mature males usually outperform mature females at spatial reasoning tasks). In the terminology of multifactorial ANOVA, we would then say that the main effects were not significant but that the Gender × Age interaction was significant. As in this hypothetical example, an interaction effect is written with a multiplication sign between the factors, and the factors are written with initial capitals (only when denoting interactions). In factorial experiments with more than two factors, three-way and sometimes even higher-order interactions are possible, but they tend to be difficult to interpret. We'll give you some tips about the interpretation of interactions towards the end of this chapter.

The analysis described in this chapter is based on the assumption that the scores are all statistically independent of one another. If scores across one or more of the factors are not independent, usually because they represent repeated measures taken from the same group of individuals, then you require a slightly different procedure, which we'll describe in chapter 11.

10.2 DATA INPUT

The data that you're going to analyse come from the experiment by Corston and Colman (1996) outlined in section 9.2. It was slightly more complex than we revealed in that section. In fact, it was a factorial experiment with two independent variables: gender (of the experimental participants or subjects) and audience condition. Both men and women students attempted to use a mouse pointer to track a small square as it moved erratically around a computer screen. The men and women who participated in the experiment were randomly assigned to treatment conditions in which they performed the task either alone, in the presence of a female audience, or in the presence of a male audience. There were therefore six treatment conditions in all:

WA: women alone
WFA: women with a female audience
WMA: women with a male audience
MA: men alone
MFA: men with a female audience
MMA: men with a male audience

Twelve women and twelve men were assigned randomly to each of the three audience conditions, and the percentages of time on target were as shown in Table 10.1.

Table 10.1   Gender and audience effects

Participant	WA	WFA	WMA	MA	MFA	MMA
1	31.4	41.0	16.2	28.8	53.2	25.2
2	2.8	46.0	21.8	31.6	48.6	7.4
3	34.8	54.0	26.8	45.4	34.0	15.6
4	27.0	36.4	23.2	37.8	66.2	32.2
5	9.8	50.4	40.8	26.4	47.4	45.6
6	24.4	31.0	12.0	26.8	24.6	45.8
7	18.4	47.2	13.6	31.0	52.4	58.6
8	14.2	51.4	16.0	19.4	39.8	56.4
9	21.0	45.8	35.2	55.6	45.6	47.8
10	20.2	40.0	22.2	72.2	44.4	64.0
11	12.2	45.8	25.4	49.2	52.6	38.4
12	12.2	25.8	2.8	47.0	46.8	55.6

The tracking scores of both women and men look higher in the female audience conditions than in the alone and male audience conditions, but statistical analysis is required to determine whether the differences between the means are statistically significant, and whether the Gender × Audience interaction is statistically significant. Here's how to compute a two-way ANOVA.

The data must be entered into the Data Editor in a single column, with a grouping variable in the first column to indicate whether each score comes from a woman or a man and another grouping variable in the second column to indicate to which of the three audience conditions it belongs. We introduced the idea behind grouping variables in section 6.2. Here's how you should enter the data (there are only 72 scores; it won't take you very long).

◆ If you've restarted SPSS and the "What would you like to do?" dialog box has opened, then click the radio button beside **Type in data**, followed by **OK**.

◆ Make sure that the Data Editor is empty, then click the **Variable View** tab at the bottom of the Data Editor and in the **Name** column, type in the name **gender** for the first variable, **audience** for the second, and **score** for the third. (If you've forgotten how to name variables, then read section 2.3 again.)

◆ Now define the value labels 1 and 2 of the **gender** variable. To do this, move the mouse pointer along the **gender** variable row and click inside the cell headed **Values**. Then click the grey button that appears on the right-hand side of the cell, and the Value Labels dialog box will open.

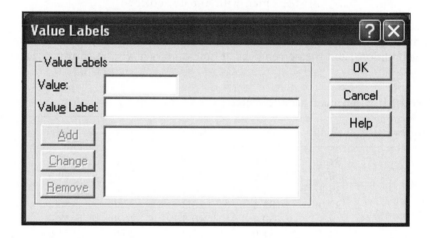

◆ Inside the text box labelled **Value**, type the numeral **1**. Click inside the text box labelled **Value Label** and type **women**. Click the **Add** button. The value label **1.00 = "women"** will appear in the list box below. To define the value 2, in the text box labelled **Value**, type the numeral **2**, then click in the text box labelled **Value Label** and type **men** and click **Add**. The value label **2.00 = "men"** will be added to the list box. Click the button labelled **OK**.

◆ Repeat the process to define the value labels of the **audience** variable. Move the mouse pointer along the **audience** variable row and click inside the cell under the **Values** heading. Then click the grey button on the right-hand side of the cell to reopen the Value Labels dialog box. Using the same procedure as before, label the values **1 = alone**, **2 = female**, and **3 = male**. The third variable, **score**, doesn't need value labels, because its values are the dependent variable scores. Click the **Data View** tab at the bottom of the Data Editor to get back to the data input window.

◆ Back in the data input window, three variables should be properly named. Now key the data from the table above into the appropriate columns of the Data Editor. There are 36 women and 36 men, so you will be using the first 72 rows of the Data Editor. All the data from table 10.1 should be entered and set out as follows (we show you only the first 16 rows):

	gender	audience	score
1	1	1	31.40
2	1	1	2.80
3	1	1	34.80
4	1	1	27.00
5	1	1	9.80
6	1	1	24.40
7	1	1	18.40
8	1	1	14.20
9	1	1	21.00
10	1	1	20.20
11	1	1	12.20
12	1	1	12.20
13	1	2	41.00
14	1	2	46.00
15	1	2	54.00
16	1	2	36.40

genaud.sav [DataSet1] - SPSS Data Editor
File Edit View Data Transform Analyze Graphs
1 : gender   1

◆ Save the data for future reference by following the procedure described in section 2.7. Call the file **genaud.sav**.

10.3 ANALYSIS

The procedure for analysing the data is not difficult, especially now that you are familiar with the general principles.

◆ Click **Analyze** in the menu bar near the top of the Data Editor. In the drop-down menu that appears, select **General Linear Model**.

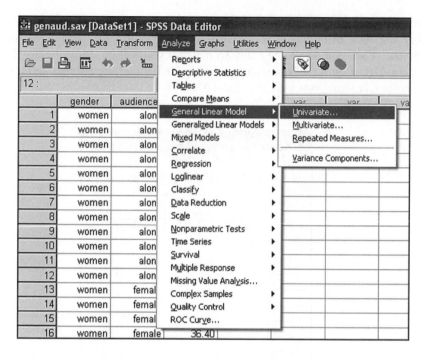

◆ Click **Univariate...** in the submenu, and the Univariate dialog box will open.

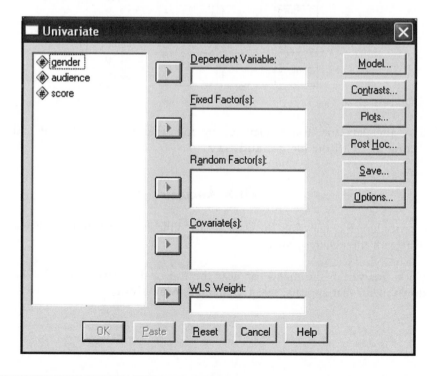

◆ In the Univariate dialog box, you have to tell SPSS that **score** is the dependent variable and that **gender** and **audience** are factors. Click **score** on the left and move it into the box labelled **Dependent Variable** by clicking the top arrow button. Then click **gender** on the left and move it to the box labelled **Fixed Factor(s)** by clicking the arrow button pointing to that box. Gender is a fixed factor because it includes all levels of the factor to which the results are intended to apply – male and female are not merely a sample of levels from the gender factor (we'll explain this further in the following paragraph). Click **audience** on the left and move it into the same **Fixed Factor(s)** box by clicking the arrow button pointing to that box.

◆ If you had any factors with levels that were merely a sample from the range of levels to which you wanted your results to apply – for example, 6-year-old, 10-year-old, and 14-year-old children, when you wanted your results to apply to other age groups not sampled – then you would put them in the **Random Factor(s)** box. If you were carrying out analysis of covariance (ANCOVA), you would put your covariate variables in the box labelled **Covariate(s)**. If you were performing a weighted least-squares analysis, you would put the variable listing the weights in the box labelled **WLS Weight**.

◆ If you wanted a customized statistical model, you could click **Model...**, and a sub-dialog box would open in which you could specify the desired model. The default is a full factorial model, with all main effects and all factor-by-factor inter-actions included. This is the usual form of ANOVA, and you should not change it unless you know what you're doing. If you wanted to include a priori tests for dif-ferences between levels of one or both factors, you could click **Contrast** to open a sub-dialog box in which you could specify the a priori contrasts that you wanted.

◆ We think it's always a good idea to plot an interaction graph, to help to interpret it if it is significant, so click **Plots...** and the Univariate: Profile Plots sub-dialog box will open.

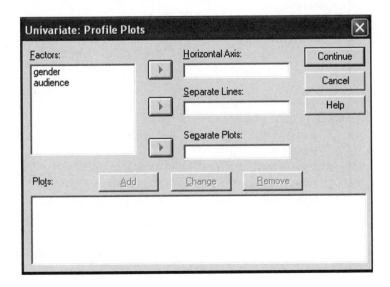

◆ The most logical plot would have the three audience conditions along the horizontal axis and separate lines on the plot for male and female students who served as experimental participants or subjects. It is usually best practice to reserve the vertical axis for values of the dependent variable. Click the factor name **audience** on the left and move it to the box labelled **Horizontal Axis** by clicking the top arrow button. Click the factor name **gender** on the left and move it to the box labelled **Separate Lines** by clicking the arrow button pointing to that box. Click **Add**, and the two factors will appear in the list box at the bottom. Click **Continue**.

◆ Back in the Univariate dialog box, click **Post Hoc...** and the Univariate: Post Hoc Multiple Comparisons for Observed Means sub-dialog box will open. We made some general comments on the various types of post hoc or a posteriori multiple comparison tests in section 9.3, and there's no need to repeat them here, but do review them if you wish. A multiple comparison test makes no sense on a factor such as gender that has only two levels, because a significant main effect for such a factor does not require further analysis, but if you have a significant main effect for audience, which has three levels, you will want to know where the differences lie, so click the factor **audience** on the left, use the arrow button to move it to the box labelled **Post Hoc Tests for**, then select **Tukey** by clicking its check box. Click **Continue**.

◆ Back in the Univariate dialog box, you could if you wished click **Save...** to save predicted values, residuals, or diagnostic statistics, but these are not often required. Click **Options...** and the Univariate: Options sub-dialog box will open.

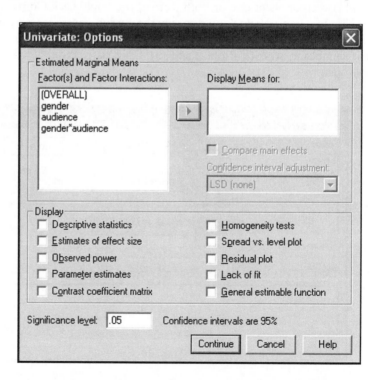

◆ It is always useful to have means and standard deviations, so in the Options sub-dialog box click the check box next to **Descriptive statistics** to put a tick there. Also click the box next to **Estimates of effect size**. You could also ask for observed power, homogeneity tests, and various other things, and you could change the significance level from the default of .05, but we won't ask for those right now. At the top of the Options box you could ask for Estimated Marginal Means (EMM) to be displayed, by moving the variables to the right-hand box **Display Means for**. This is used when you want to adjust the means to remove the effect of a covariate. When you haven't got a covariate, then the EMM will be the same as the means from your sample, which are displayed using the **Descriptive statistics** option at the bottom of the Options box. For now, just click **Continue**.

◆ Back for the last time in the Univariate dialog box, click **OK**, and the results will be displayed in the Output Viewer. To print a hard copy of the output, follow the procedure described in section 3.2. To print a selection of the output, first click or shift-click the desired names in the panel on the left, or click the tables themselves, then use the procedure described in section 3.3.

10.4 RESULTS

Univariate Analysis of Variance

Between-Subjects Factors

		Value Label	N
gender	1	women	36
	2	men	36
audience	1	alone	24
	2	female	24
	3	male	24

Descriptive Statistics

Dependent Variable: score

gender	audience	Mean	Std. Deviation	N
women	alone	19.0333	9.36602	12
	female	42.9000	8.44727	12
	male	21.3333	10.30140	12
	Total	27.7556	14.21999	36
men	alone	39.2667	15.08144	12
	female	46.3000	10.42637	12
	male	41.0500	17.80564	12
	Total	42.2056	14.64439	36
Total	alone	29.1500	16.04778	24
	female	44.6000	9.44108	24
	male	31.1917	17.42966	24
	Total	34.9806	16.07280	72

Tests of Between-Subjects Effects

Dependent Variable: score

Source	Type III Sum of Squares	df	Mean Square	F	Sig.	Partial Eta Squared
Corrected Model	8239.403[a]	5	1647.881	10.766	.000	.449
Intercept	88102.027	1	88102.027	575.581	.000	.897
gender	3758.445	1	3758.445	24.554	.000	.271
audience	3381.234	2	1690.617	11.045	.000	.251
gender * audience	1099.723	2	549.862	3.592	.033	.098
Error	10102.370	66	153.066			
Total	106443.800	72				
Corrected Total	18341.773	71				

a. R Squared = .449 (Adjusted R Squared = .407)

Post Hoc Tests

audience

Multiple Comparisons

Dependent Variable: score
Tukey HSD

(I) audience	(J) audience	Mean Difference (I-J)	Std. Error	Sig.	95% Confidence Interval	
					Lower Bound	Upper Bound
alone	female	-15.4500*	3.57149	.000	-24.0134	-6.8866
	male	-2.0417	3.57149	.836	-10.6050	6.5217
female	alone	15.4500*	3.57149	.000	6.8866	24.0134
	male	13.4083*	3.57149	.001	4.8450	21.9717
male	alone	2.0417	3.57149	.836	-6.5217	10.6050
	female	-13.4083*	3.57149	.001	-21.9717	-4.8450

Based on observed means.

*. The mean difference is significant at the .05 level.

Homogeneous Subsets

score

Tukey HSD[a,b]

audience	N	Subset	
		1	2
alone	24	29.1500	
male	24	31.1917	
female	24		44.6000
Sig.		.836	1.000

Means for groups in homogeneous subsets are displayed.
Based on Type III Sum of Squares
The error term is Mean Square(Error) = 153.066.

a. Uses Harmonic Mean Sample Size = 24.000.

b. Alpha = .05.

Profile Plots

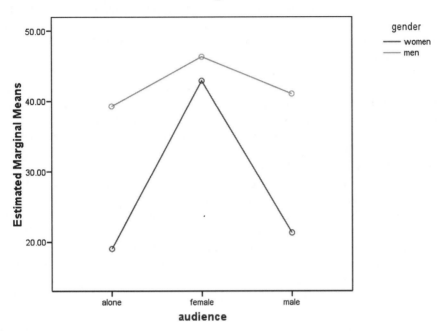

Estimated Marginal Means of score

The first table of the output, labelled Between-Subjects Factors, merely summarizes the factors, showing how they were labelled and how many scores there are in each group.

The second table, labelled Descriptive Statistics, shows the two means for the gender factor (women total, men total) and the three means for the audience factor (total alone, total female, total male) together with their standard deviations. The means and SD for the interactions, and for the overall total, are also shown. You should "eyeball" these means to get a feel for them and any possible patterns and differences.

The next table, labelled Tests of Between-Subjects Effects, is a standard ANOVA table with a few additions. The first column lists the sources of variation analysed. The main body of the table lists, among other things, the sum of squares, degrees of freedom (df), mean square, value of F, significance of F (Sig.), and the effect size Partial Eta Squared, of each of the factors individually and also of the Gender × Audience interaction (which appears in the table as GENDER*AUDIENCE). It is clear that both of the main effects are significant at .000 (which you should interpret to mean that p is less than .001) and that the Gender × Audience interaction is also significant at .033.

The last two tables, under the general heading Post Hoc Tests, display the results of the multiple comparisons on the audience factor, using the Tukey-HSD test that you selected. We explained the meaning of these slightly mysterious tables in section 9.4. In this case, they show that mean time on target was significantly greater in the female audience condition than in the alone or the male audience condition, and that no other pairwise differences on levels of the audience factor were significant.

The last item of output is the interaction graph showing mean time on target of the women and men students in each of the three audience conditions, and it is useful having this plot, because the interaction is significant and it needs to be interpreted. We'll tell you more about drawing and editing graphs in section 15.4.

The usual way of reporting these results is to say something like the following. "The mean score of the male subjects ($M = 42.21$) was higher than the mean score of the female subjects ($M = 27.76$), and this difference was significant: $F(1, 66) = 24.55$, $p < .001$, partial $\eta^2 = .27$. The main effect of audience condition was also significant, $F(2, 66) = 11.05$, $p < .001$, partial $\eta^2 = .25$, with the highest scores in the female audience condition ($M = 44.60$) compared with the male audience ($M = 31.19$) and the alone condition ($M = 29.15$). A posteriori Tukey-HSD tests showed that the mean for the female audience condition was significantly higher than the means for the other two audience conditions ($p < .05$, two-tailed) and that no other pairwise differences on levels of this factor were significant. Finally, the Gender × Audience interaction was significant, $F(2, 66) = 3.59$, $p < .05$, partial $\eta^2 = .09$."

Interactions are notoriously difficult to interpret, and explaining what they mean is an art as well as a science. We find it helpful to think about interactions as follows. A main effect is a significant difference between two or more means; a two-way interaction is a significant difference between two or more *differences* between two or more means; a three-way interaction is a significant difference between two or more differences between two or more differences between two or more means; and so on, but from that point on the idea begins to become too complex to grasp. It is always helpful to examine interaction graphs. In the data you have just analysed, the differences between the mean scores of men and women differ quite sharply from one audience condition to the next, so there are differences between these differences, and that is why the interaction effect is significant – the interpretation is fairly obvious from the graph.

In the article from which the data were taken, the interaction was interpreted as follows: "With a female audience, female subjects' scores were similar to those of male subjects, but when working alone or in the presence of a male audience, female subjects' scores were vastly worse than those of male subjects" (Corston & Colman, 1996, pp. 166–167). Another way of interpreting the interaction would be to say that female audiences had a positive effect, especially on the performance of women, but male audiences had roughly the same effect as no audience at all. In other words, the male spectator, who was in fact one of the authors of this book, functioned like a nebbish. According to a popular definition of this Yiddish word, when a nebbish enters a room, you feel as if someone has just left.

◆ Click **File** in the menu bar near the top of the Output Viewer, followed by **Close**, and when a dialog box appears asking whether you want to save the contents of the Output Viewer, click **Yes** or **No**, and if **Yes**, follow the procedure in section 2.7. Back in the data entry window of the Data Editor, if you want to go straight on to the next chapter, click **File** in the menu bar and select **New**, then click **Data**. If you want to exit from SPSS, then click **File** and then **Exit**. If you have not saved the input data, a dialog box will appear asking whether you wish to do so, and you should click **Yes** and save the input data under the filename **genaud.sav**, because you'll need them again in section 15.4 when we tell you more about drawing and editing graphs.

11 Repeated-measures Analysis of Variance

11.1 BACKGROUND

One-way ANOVA with repeated measures is, in effect, an extension of the paired-samples t test, described in chapter 7, the difference being that the means of more than two related samples are compared simultaneously. Data that require analysis using this procedure most often arise when three or more measurements of a variable are taken from a single group of individuals at different times. The situation is slightly more complicated when a multifactorial ANOVA includes one or more repeated-measures factors. The data that you're going to analyse in this chapter, for example, come from a 2 × 3 factorial experiment in which one factor was a between-subjects factor and the other was a within-subjects factor; that is, a repeated-measures factor. Experimental designs of this type are sometimes called mixed designs or split-plot designs.

If we show you how to analyse the data from this two-way mixed ANOVA with repeated measures on one factor, then you shouldn't find it difficult to adapt the technique for one-way repeated-measures designs, which are simpler, or for multi-factorial designs with repeated measures on more than one factor, which are more complicated but involve merely duplicating, for each repeated-measures factor, the procedure that we'll describe for the single repeated-measures factor in this chapter. It should be fairly obvious once you've analysed the data below. But please note that you will not be able to perform repeated-measures ANOVA unless your version includes the SPSS Advanced Models (previously called Advanced Statistics) option.

Colman (1982, pp. 184–190) reported an experiment designed in part to invest-igate framing effects on cooperative decisions in social dilemmas. A social dilemma is a decision problem in which members of a group each face a choice between a cooperative choice that benefits the group as a whole and an uncooperative choice that benefits the individual at the expense of the group, and the pursuit of individual self-interest by every group member leaves everyone worse off than if they had all acted cooperatively. In one treatment condition the social dilemma was framed as an abstract decision problem, and in another it was framed as a lifelike decision prob-lem, but the two versions were strategically equivalent, the only difference being the framing or description of the dilemma to the group members. In both framing con-ditions, the group members made a series of 30 decisions, which were divided into three blocks of 10 decisions each. The total numbers of cooperative choices in each of the 20 groups were as shown in Table 11.1.

The unit of analysis is the group, so think of each of the 20 groups as a separate data source, each group being able to make between zero and 30 cooperative choices (10 decisions for each of three decision makers) in each trial block.

11.2 DATA INPUT

For repeated-measures ANOVA, the scores are not entered into a single column of the Data Editor, as would be required for a standard randomized-groups ANOVA such as the one we showed you in chapter 10. The data must be entered so that the

Table 11.1   Social dilemmas

	Group	Trial Block 1	Trial Block 2	Trial Block 3
	1	11	8	4
	2	12	10	9
	3	20	18	13
	4	14	9	3
Abstract	5	14	6	11
	6	13	6	7
	7	10	10	7
	8	9	8	4
	9	14	16	11
	10	12	8	5
	11	7	5	6
	12	8	5	6
	13	7	3	1
	14	3	0	0
Lifelike	15	5	0	0
	16	14	9	10
	17	5	6	7
	18	7	2	1
	19	12	7	4
	20	11	8	5

repeated measures from each case appear in a single row, as they do in Table 11.1. Usually each row represents an individual participant or subject, but in this data set each row corresponds to one of the 20 groups. The different levels of the between-subjects factor(s) are set out one below the other, again as in the table above, and a grouping variable is used to indicate to which group each row of scores belongs. Here's what you need to do.

◆ If you've restarted SPSS and the "What would you like to do?" dialog box has opened, then click the radio button beside **Type in data**, followed by **OK**.
◆ Name four variables by clicking the **Variable View** tab at the bottom-left of the Data Editor and typing the names **group**, **block1**, **block2**, and **block3** in the first four rows of the **Name** column.
◆ Now define the value labels 1 and 2 of the **group** variable, because it is the grouping variable. To do this, move the mouse pointer along the **group** variable row and click inside the cell headed **Values**. Then click the grey button that appears on the right-hand side of the cell, and the Value Labels dialog box will open.

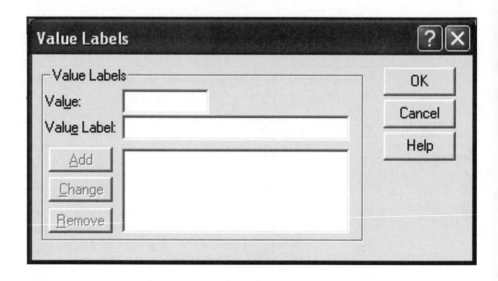

◆ In the text box labelled **Value**, type the numeral **1**. Click inside the text box labelled **Value Label** and type **abstract**. Click the **Add** button. The value label **1.00** = "abstract" will appear in the list box below. To define the value 2, in the text box labelled **Value**, type the numeral **2**, then click in the text box labelled **Value Label** and type **lifelike** and click **Add**. The value label **2.00** = "lifelike" will be added to the list box. The other variables contain data scores and don't need value labels. Click the button labelled **OK**. Click the **Data View** tab at the bottom of the Data Editor to get back to the data input window.
◆ Four variables should now be labelled in the data input window. Key the data from Table 11.1 into the appropriate columns of the Data Editor. There are 10 groups assigned to the abstract treatment condition and 10 to the lifelike treatment condition, so you will be typing into the first 20 rows of the Data Editor. The data should be set out in the Data Editor as follows:

	group	block1	block2	block3
1	1.00	11.00	8.00	4.00
2	1.00	12.00	10.00	9.00
3	1.00	20.00	18.00	13.00
4	1.00	14.00	9.00	3.00
5	1.00	14.00	6.00	11.00
6	1.00	13.00	6.00	7.00

11	2.00	7.00	5.00	6.00
12	2.00	8.00	5.00	6.00
13	2.00	7.00	3.00	1.00
14	2.00	3.00	.00	.00
15	2.00	5.00	.00	.00
16	2.00	14.00	9.00	10.00

◆ Save the data for future reference by following the procedure described in section 2.7. Call the file **dilemmas.sav**.

11.3 ANALYSIS

Performing repeated-measures ANOVA is easy, provided that you have the SPSS Advanced Models (previously called Advanced Statistics) option.

◆ Click **Analyze** in the menu bar near the top of the Data Editor, and in the drop-down menu that appears select **General Linear Model**.

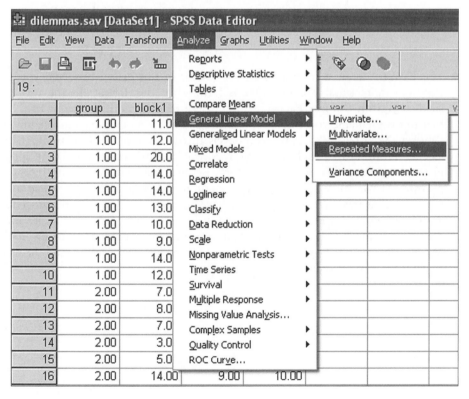

◆ Click **Repeated Measures...** in the submenu, and the Repeated Measures Define Factor(s) dialog box will open. If you have only the Base System of SPSS, this command won't appear on the drop-down submenu, and you won't be able to select it.

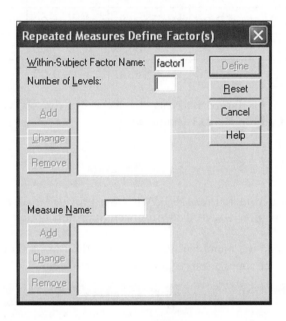

◆ You have to define a repeated-measures factor in this dialog box, and you can choose a more suitable name for this factor than the default. In the text box labelled **Within-Subject Factor Name**, delete **factor1**, and type **trials**. Note that this is the name you create for a factor and is not an existing variable in your data set. Now tell SPSS how many levels this factor has. Click in the text box labelled **Number of Levels** and type **3**. Now click **Add**, and **trials(3)** will appear in the list of repeated-measures factors. Because you have only one repeated-measures factor, there is no more work to do in this dialog box. If you had more repeated-measures factors, you would have to go through the same procedure again, adding more factors to the list in this box. If you were using a multivariate design with more than one dependent variable, you would need to fill in the **Measure Name** text box lower down, but for now just click **Define**, and the main Repeated Measures dialog box will appear.

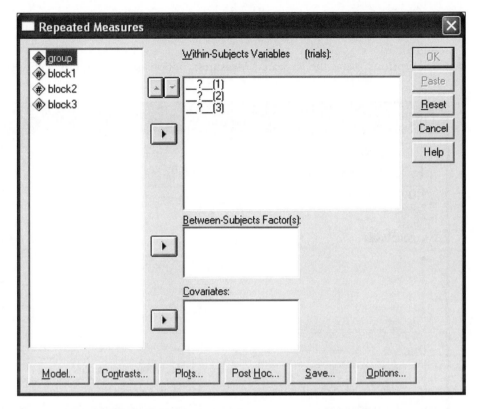

◆ In the Repeated Measures dialog box, the box labelled **Within-Subjects Variables** on the right is obviously begging for three items of information: it has _?_ repeated three times within it. Move **block1**, **block2**, and **block3** in that order from the source box on the left to the **Within-Subjects Variables** box on the right (now helpfully labelled **trials**) by clicking to highlight each of them and then clicking the black arrow button between them. Properly speaking, these are the three levels of your within-subjects factor, so the order is crucial.

◆ Move **group** from the left to the box labelled **Between-Subjects Factor(s)** by clicking it and then clicking the appropriate arrow button. If you were carrying out a repeated-measures analysis of covariance (ANCOVA), then at this point you would have to put your covariate or covariates in the box labelled **Covariates**.

◆ If you wanted a customized statistical model, you could click **Model...**, and a sub-dialog box would open in which you could specify the desired model. The default is a full factorial model, with all main effects and all factor-by-factor interactions included, and this is the usual form of ANOVA. If you wanted to include an a priori test for differences between levels of one or both factors, you could click **Contrasts...** to open a sub-dialog box in which you could specify the a priori contrasts that you wanted (we mentioned these in section 9.3). If you had some between-subjects factors with three or more levels, you could click **Post Hoc** to perform a posteriori multiple comparisons on any significant main effects (we discussed these at some length in section 9.3). If you wanted a graph of the results, you could click **Plots...**, and if you wanted to save predicted values, residuals, or diagnostic statistics you could click **Save...**, but these are seldom required.

◆ Click **Options...** and the Repeated Measures: Options sub-dialog box will open.

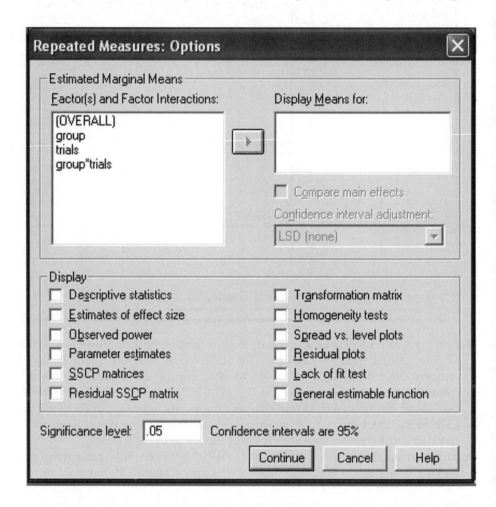

◆ It is always useful to have means and standard deviations, so in the Options sub-dialog box click the check box next to **Descriptive statistics** to put a tick there. Also click the box next to **Estimates of effect size**. You could also ask for observed power, homogeneity tests, and various other things, and you could change the significance level from the default of .05, but we won't ask for those right now.

◆ At the top of the Options box you could ask for Estimated Marginal Means (EMM) to be displayed, by moving the variables to the right-hand box **Display Means for**. This is used when you want to adjust the means to remove the effect of a covariate. When you haven't got a covariate, the EMM will be the same as the means from your sample, which are displayed using the **Descriptive statistics** option at the bottom of the Options box. It is also possible to get a posteriori or post-hoc multiple comparisons for the within-subjects factor here, so in the Repeated Measures: Options sub-dialog box click the factor **trials** on the left and move it to the box labelled **Display Means for** on the right by clicking the arrow button and tick the box next to **Compare main effects**. Now just click **Continue**.

◆ Back once again in the Repeated Measures dialog box, click **OK**, and the results will be displayed in the Output Viewer.

◆ To print a hard copy of the output, follow the procedure described in section 3.2. To print a selection of the output, first click or shift-click the desired names in the panel on the left, or click the tables themselves, then use the procedure described in section 3.3.

11.4 RESULTS

General Linear Model

Within-Subjects Factors

Measure: MEASURE_1

trials	Dependent Variable
1	block1
2	block2
3	block3

Between-Subjects Factors

		Value Label	N
group	1.00	abstract	10
	2.00	lifelike	10

Descriptive Statistics

	group	Mean	Std. Deviation	N
block1	abstract	12.9000	3.03498	10
	lifelike	7.9000	3.44642	10
	Total	10.4000	4.07043	20
block2	abstract	9.9000	4.01248	10
	lifelike	4.5000	3.17105	10
	Total	7.2000	4.47919	20
block3	abstract	7.4000	3.47051	10
	lifelike	4.0000	3.39935	10
	Total	5.7000	3.77108	20

Multivariate Tests[b]

Effect		Value	F	Hypothesis df	Error df	Sig.	Partial Eta Squared
trials	Pillai's Trace	.769	28.373[a]	2.000	17.000	.000	.769
	Wilks' Lambda	.231	28.373[a]	2.000	17.000	.000	.769
	Hotelling's Trace	3.338	28.373[a]	2.000	17.000	.000	.769
	Roy's Largest Root	3.338	28.373[a]	2.000	17.000	.000	.769
trials * group	Pillai's Trace	.144	1.435[a]	2.000	17.000	.265	.144
	Wilks' Lambda	.856	1.435[a]	2.000	17.000	.265	.144
	Hotelling's Trace	.169	1.435[a]	2.000	17.000	.265	.144
	Roy's Largest Root	.169	1.435[a]	2.000	17.000	.265	.144

a. Exact statistic

b.
   Design: Intercept+group
   Within Subjects Design: trials

Mauchly's Test of Sphericity[b]

Measure: MEASURE_1

Within Subjects Effect	Mauchly's W	Approx. Chi-Square	df	Sig.	Epsilon[a] Greenhouse-Geisser	Huynh-Feldt	Lower-bound
trials	.989	.194	2	.907	.989	1.000	.500

Tests the null hypothesis that the error covariance matrix of the orthonormalized transformed dependent variables is proportional to an identity matrix.

a. May be used to adjust the degrees of freedom for the averaged tests of significance. Corrected tests are displayed in the Tests of Within-Subjects Effects table.

b.
   Design: Intercept+group
   Within Subjects Design: trials

Tests of Within-Subjects Effects

Measure: MEASURE_1

Source		Type III Sum of Squares	df	Mean Square	F	Sig.	Partial Eta Squared
trials	Sphericity Assumed	230.533	2	115.267	32.351	.000	.643
	Greenhouse-Geisser	230.533	1.978	116.577	32.351	.000	.643
	Huynh-Feldt	230.533	2.000	115.267	32.351	.000	.643
	Lower-bound	230.533	1.000	230.533	32.351	.000	.643
trials * group	Sphericity Assumed	11.200	2	5.600	1.572	.222	.080
	Greenhouse-Geisser	11.200	1.978	5.664	1.572	.222	.080
	Huynh-Feldt	11.200	2.000	5.600	1.572	.222	.080
	Lower-bound	11.200	1.000	11.200	1.572	.226	.080
Error(trials)	Sphericity Assumed	128.267	36	3.563			
	Greenhouse-Geisser	128.267	35.595	3.603			
	Huynh-Feldt	128.267	36.000	3.563			
	Lower-bound	128.267	18.000	7.126			

112

Tests of Within-Subjects Contrasts

Measure: MEASURE_1

Source	trials	Type III Sum of Squares	df	Mean Square	F	Sig.	Partial Eta Squared
trials	Linear	220.900	1	220.900	56.240	.000	.758
	Quadratic	9.633	1	9.633	3.012	.100	.143
trials * group	Linear	6.400	1	6.400	1.629	.218	.083
	Quadratic	4.800	1	4.800	1.501	.236	.077
Error(trials)	Linear	70.700	18	3.928			
	Quadratic	57.567	18	3.198			

Tests of Between-Subjects Effects

Measure: MEASURE_1

Transformed Variable: Average

Source	Type III Sum of Squares	df	Mean Square	F	Sig.	Partial Eta Squared
Intercept	3619.267	1	3619.267	127.906	.000	.877
group	317.400	1	317.400	11.217	.004	.384
Error	509.333	18	28.296			

Estimated Marginal Means

1. trials

Estimates

Measure: MEASURE_1

trials	Mean	Std. Error	95% Confidence Interval	
			Lower Bound	Upper Bound
1	10.400	.726	8.875	11.925
2	7.200	.809	5.501	8.899
3	5.700	.768	4.086	7.314

Pairwise Comparisons

Measure: MEASURE_1

(I) trials	(J) trials	Mean Difference (I-J)	Std. Error	Sig.[a]	95% Confidence Interval for Difference[a]	
					Lower Bound	Upper Bound
1	2	3.200*	.573	.000	1.995	4.405
	3	4.700*	.627	.000	3.383	6.017
2	1	-3.200*	.573	.000	-4.405	-1.995
	3	1.500*	.589	.020	.262	2.738
3	1	-4.700*	.627	.000	-6.017	-3.383
	2	-1.500*	.589	.020	-2.738	-.262

Based on estimated marginal means

*. The mean difference is significant at the .05 level.

a. Adjustment for multiple comparisons: Least Significant Difference (equivalent to no adjustments).

Multivariate Tests

	Value	F	Hypothesis df	Error df	Sig.	Partial Eta Squared
Pillai's trace	.769	28.373[a]	2.000	17.000	.000	.769
Wilks' lambda	.231	28.373[a]	2.000	17.000	.000	.769
Hotelling's trace	3.338	28.373[a]	2.000	17.000	.000	.769
Roy's largest root	3.338	28.373[a]	2.000	17.000	.000	.769

Each F tests the multivariate effect of trials. These tests are based on the linearly independent pairwise comparisons among the estimated marginal means.

a. Exact statistic

The output from this procedure is voluminous and slightly confusing, with much information that you don't need, but you won't find it difficult to pick out the wheat from the chaff once we've talked you through this example.

The first table in the Output Viewer, labelled **Within-Subjects Factors**, merely confirms that there is just one repeated-measures factor called TRIALS, with the three variables BLOCK1, BLOCK2, and BLOCK3 defining the three levels of the factor. The second table, labelled **Between-Subjects Factors**, confirms that there is one between-subjects factor, called GROUP, with value labels abstract and lifelike for the two levels of the factor, and $N = 10$ in each group.

The third table, **Descriptive Statistics**, gives the means and standard deviations of the table cells. The fourth table, **Multivariate Tests**, can be ignored, because the data in this analysis are univariate rather than multivariate – there is just one dependent variable, namely the number of cooperative choices per group per trial block.

The fifth table, **Mauchly's Test of Sphericity**, should not be ignored. It displays the results of a test of certain important homogeneity-of-variance assumptions about the variance–covariance matrix of the dependent variable. If the significance of Mauchly's W is small (usually taken to mean less than .05), then the assumptions are not met and an adjustment needs to be made to the degrees of freedom to draw conclusions from the ANOVA. In this case, the significance of Mauchly's W is high (.907), so the assumptions are met and no adjustments are needed.

The sixth table, **Tests of Within-Subjects Effects**, shows the sum of squares, degrees of freedom (df), mean square, F, and significance level of F (Sig.) of the repeated-measures factor (trials) and the Trials × Group interaction. In both cases, the values are given first with sphericity assumed (see the previous paragraph), and then with each of three possible adjustments to the degrees of freedom using different values of epsilon in case the sphericity assumption was not met. In this case, the sphericity assumption was met, so we may use the values with sphericity assumed and ignore the rest. For the repeated-measures factor trials, F is given as 32.351 and the significance of F as .000 (p less than .001), and for the Trials × Group interaction, F is given as 1.572 and the significance of F as $p = .222$. Most useful in this table are the partial eta squared values of the effects. These provide estimates of the sizes of these effects.

The seventh table, **Tests of Within-Subjects Contrasts**, provides estimates of the linear and curvilinear trend across levels of the repeated-measures factor (trials) and the Trials × Group interaction differences, together with associated eta squared effect size estimates. In this case the linear trend in the trials factor is significant ($F = 56.24$, $p < .001$), suggesting that the number of cooperative choices changed steadily or evenly over trial blocks, and the quadratic trend is not significant ($F = 3.01$, $p > .05$). There are no significant trends in the Trials × Group interaction differences.

The eighth table, **Tests of Between-Subjects Effects**, displays the sum of squares, degrees of freedom (df), F, significance level of F (Sig.), and η^2 effect sizes of the between-subjects factor (group). For this factor, the F ratio is given as 11.217 and the significance level as .004, with an η^2 effect size of .38.

In the **Estimated Marginal Means** that follow, the most useful information is contained in the table of **Pairwise Comparisons**. This shows that, on the repeated-measures variable Trials, each of the three means differs significantly from the other two: the mean for Trial Block 1 is significantly different from the means of Trial Blocks 2 and 3, the mean for Trial Block 2 is significantly different from the means of Trial Blocks 1 and 3, and the mean for Trial Block 3 is significantly different from the means of Trial Blocks 1 and 2. The differences are significant at the 5 per cent level, and a note below the table confirms that the multiple comparisons used the Least Significant Difference method.

In a journal article or research monograph, we would report the results of the analysis as follows. "A significant main effect due to the framing of the social dilemma was observed. The mean number of cooperative choices per trial block was higher in the Abstract framing group ($M = 10.07$) than in the Lifelike framing group ($M = 5.47$), and this difference was significant: $F(1, 18) = 11.22$, $p = .004$, partial $\eta^2 = .38$. There was a decline in the mean number of cooperative choices across trial blocks, with $M = 10.40$ in Trial Block 1, $M = 7.20$ in Trial Block 2, and $M = 5.70$ in Trial Block 3. The differences between these three means were significant: $F(2, 36) = 32.35$, $p < .001$, partial $\eta^2 = .64$, and least significant difference multiple comparisons confirm that each of the three means differs significantly from each of the others. The Trial Block × Group interaction was not significant: $F(2, 36) = 1.57$, $p > .05$."

◆ Click **File** in the menu bar near the top of the Output Viewer, followed by **Close**, and when a dialog box appears asking whether you want to save the contents of the Output Viewer, click **Yes** or **No**, and if **Yes**, follow the procedure in section 2.7. Back in the data entry window of the Data Editor, if you want to go straight on to the next chapter, click **File** in the menu bar and select **New**, then click **Data**. If you want to exit from SPSS, then click **File** and then **Exit**. If you have not saved the input data, a dialog box will appear asking whether you wish to do so, and you should click **Yes** and save the input data for future reference under the filename `dilemmas.sav`.

12 Multiple Regression

12.1 BACKGROUND

Multiple regression (or multiple linear regression analysis, to give it its full name) is an extension or generalization of a basic bivariate (two-variable) technique of linear regression that Francis Galton, half-cousin of the biologist Charles Darwin, originally put forward in a primitive form at a meeting of the Royal Institution in London, in 1877. It is a statistical technique for analysing the separate and joint influences of two or more independent variables, also called predictor variables, on a dependent variable. The general form of a multiple regression equation for k independent variables is a weighted sum:

$$Y = \beta_0 + \beta_1 X_1 + \beta_2 X_2 + \ldots + \beta_k X_k.$$

In this equation, Y is the *predicted* score on the dependent variable, each X_i is one of the independent variables, β_0 is the intercept (the value of Y when all of the $X_i = 0$), and each β_i ($i = 1$ to k) is a standardized regression coefficient indicating the relative importance of the corresponding independent or predictor variable in determining the predicted value of the dependent variable. The standardized regression coefficients are often called beta weights, because the symbol β in the equation is the lower-case letter beta, the second letter of the Greek alphabet. Sometimes the symbol B is used instead of β, especially for unstandardized regression coefficients, and it is in fact an upper-case Greek beta, although it looks identical to the second letter of the Roman alphabet. Regression analysis calculates the intercept and regression coefficients so as to provide the best-fitting linear equation according to the least-squares criterion; that is, such that the sum of the squared deviations of the predicted scores from the observed scores is minimized to give the most accurate prediction. The multiple regression procedure is one of the largest and most complex in SPSS, but that is no cause for alarm, although it does make it difficult for us to summarize the procedure briefly. We'll deal with it as straightforwardly as we can without omitting too many important details.

The data in Table 12.1 are taken from the first full-scale Research Assessment Exercise carried out by the Universities Funding Council (UFC) in the United Kingdom in 1992 (Universities Funding Council, 1993). We've chosen the ratings of anthropology departments, because there were only 17 of them in the assessment exercise, and it shouldn't take you too long to key in the data. But it will take a few minutes, so do be patient – you need a reasonable amount of data to perform a meaningful multiple regression analysis.

The first column simply labels each of the British universities that had anthropology departments in 1992 – we've omitted their names to save their blushes. The second column is the dependent variable, namely the ratings of research performance awarded by the UFC on a scale from 1 (worst) to 5 (best). The following five columns contain the performance indicators that were used in the Research Assessment Exercise and that you are about to subject to multiple regression analysis:

Table 12.1   Research assessment data

Univ	Rating	Staffing	Pubs	Articles	ABRC	Grants
1	4	6.75	13.56	2.52	13464	2856
2	5	28.25	21.29	4.46	21401	9561
3	4	10.50	13.08	3.36	95	582
4	4	13.00	9.15	1.42	16050	5814
5	3	7.50	10.17	1.73	716	8161
6	5	19.75	10.22	1.77	13070	10706
7	5	19.50	15.17	1.67	2053	3562
8	5	20.75	16.17	2.55	6680	5608
9	5	12.25	16.67	1.80	3384	2994
10	5	29.00	13.96	2.58	13261	26351
11	2	4.50	25.38	3.22	3678	15853
12	4	10.50	9.75	.76	472	26149
13	4	14.50	11.35	1.72	6772	7814
14	4	13.25	11.47	1.47	6699	346
15	3	6.00	5.50	2.33	6573	1144
16	1	4.50	2.89	.22	0	0
17	3	17.25	7.48	.87	0	1755

Staffing: The average number of staff members in the department over the assessment period (1988 to 1992)

Pubs: The average number of publications of all types per staff member over the assessment period (not time spent by staff members in public houses, a performance indicator that the UFC overlooked completely)

Articles: The average number of articles in academic journals per staff member over the assessment period

ABRC: Advisory Board for Research Councils, that is, research income from government research councils per staff member over the assessment period

Grants: Other external research income per staff member over the assessment period

How well can we predict a department's rating on the basis of its scores on the five independent variables? What was the relative importance of the various performance indicators in determining the ratings? To answer questions such as these you need to perform a multiple regression analysis as follows.

12.2 DATA INPUT

The data input is quite straightforward, and it is similar to data input for other procedures in SPSS, so it will not cause you problems.

◆ If you've restarted SPSS and the "What would you like to do?" dialog box has opened, then click the radio button beside **Type in data**, followed by **OK**.

◆ Begin by clicking the **Variable View** tab at the bottom of the Data Editor and naming the first six variables in the **Name** column **rating**, **staffing**, **pubs**, **articles**, **abrc**, and **grants** in that order. None of these variables is a grouping variable, so there are no values to define. Click the **Data View** tab at the bottom of the window, and in the data input window of the Data Editor six variables should now be labelled.

◆ Key the data from Table 12.1 into the first 17 rows using the procedure described in section 2.4.

◆ Save the data for future reference by following the procedure described in section 2.7. Call this data file **regress.sav**.

12.3 ANALYSIS

Performing a multiple regression analysis is quite a long and complex process, but it isn't particularly difficult once you know what you're doing.

◆ Click **Analyze** in the menu bar near the top of the Data Editor and select **Regression**.

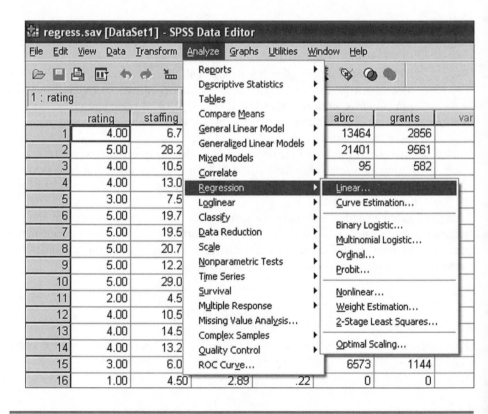

◆ Click **Linear...** in the submenu, and the Linear Regression dialog box will open.

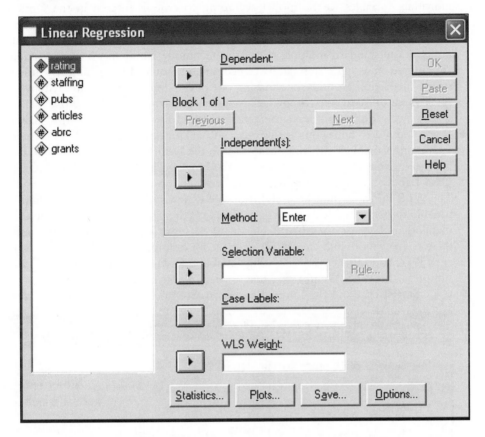

◆ Move the variable name **rating** to the **Dependent** box, because it is the dependent variable, and all the other variable names to the **Independent(s)** box, because they are all independent or predictor variables. To move a variable from the source box on the left to one of the boxes on the right, click it if it isn't already highlighted, and then click the arrow button pointing to the desired destination box. To move a whole group of variable names together, click the one at the top of the group, then while holding the shift key down click the bottom one in the group. The whole group will be selected, and if you then click the arrow button they will all move together.

◆ If you wanted to use a method other than standard (forced entry) multiple regression, which is the default and is called **Enter**, you could click the arrow to the right of the box labelled **Method** and click one of the alternatives in the drop-down menu that would open. The alternatives are **Stepwise**, which adds and removes variables from the model according to criteria entered in the Options dialog box; **Remove**, which begins with all variables in the model and then removes variables *en bloc*; **Backward**, which removes individual variables from the model according to criteria entered in the Options dialog box until a model is reached from which no more are eligible for removal; and **Forward**, which adds individual variables to the model according to criteria entered in the Options dialog box until a model is reached from which no more are eligible for entry. The least controversial of these techniques, and the most suitable for most purposes, is the standard multiple regression technique **Enter** in which all variables are entered in a single step, and we recommend that you use it unless you have strong theoretical grounds for choosing one of the stepwise procedures (**Stepwise**, **Backward**, or **Forward**). **Stepwise** is popular, and you could choose this method simply by clicking it, but leave the default method **Enter** selected for this analysis.

◆ If you wanted to limit your analysis to a subset of cases, you could have included a grouping variable identifying these cases in the Data Editor, and you would now have to move that grouping variable to the box labelled **Selection Variable**. The **Case Labels** box is for identifying certain points on a scatterplot of the results. The **WLS** button would be useful if one of your variables had been a weighting variable for weighted least-squares analysis, attaching more weight to some cases than others because they had been measured more accurately and you wanted them to have more influence in the analysis, for example, in which case you could click **WLS** and transfer the weighting variable that you had entered into the Data Editor to the **WLS Weight** box that appears if you click the **WLS** button.

◆ Click **Statistics...** and the Linear Regression: Statistics sub-dialog box will open.

◆ In this Linear Regression: Statistics sub-dialog box you could click check boxes to select various additional statistics that you wished to be displayed with the output. The two items that are selected by default and are required for virtually all multiple regressions are **Estimates**, which are the regression coefficients themselves, and **Model fit** statistics, which include R^2, the coefficient of determination, which is the proportion of variance in the dependent variable that is explained by the regression equation or model. Among the additional options are **Confidence intervals**, the 95 per cent confidence intervals for the regression coefficients; **Covariance matrix**, a table showing the variance of each regression coefficient and the covariances between every pair of coefficients; **R squared change**, the change in R^2 that is produced by adding or deleting an independent variable (a large change shows that the variable is a good predictor of the dependent variable); **Descriptives**, the mean and standard deviation of each variable and a correlation matrix for the complete set of variables; and **Collinearity diagnostics**, including the tolerance of each variable and other statistics for diagnosing collinearity problems. The collinearity diagnostics are designed to check an assumption of multiple regression, namely that one independent variable is not a linear function of the others. At the bottom of the sub-dialog box you will find **Durbin-Watson**, the Durbin–Watson test for serial correlation of residuals, which checks another crucial assumption of multiple regression when it's performed on observations recorded sequentially or serially, namely that the residuals of consecutive observations are uncorrelated. A residual is the observed value of the dependent variable minus the value predicted by the model. If the residuals are uncorrelated, then the Durbin–Watson statistic is 2; values close to either zero or 4 indicate positive or negative correlation, respectively, and imply that the assumption is violated. Finally, there is a check box for **Casewise diagnostics** for identifying extreme scores or outliers. When you've selected the statistics you require and deselected the others (for now just select the defaults **Estimates** and **Model fit**, which are more than enough for our purposes), click **Continue**.

◆ Back in the Linear Regression dialog box, if you want the output to include scatterplots of various kinds, click **Plots...** and the Linear Regression: Plots sub-dialog box will open.

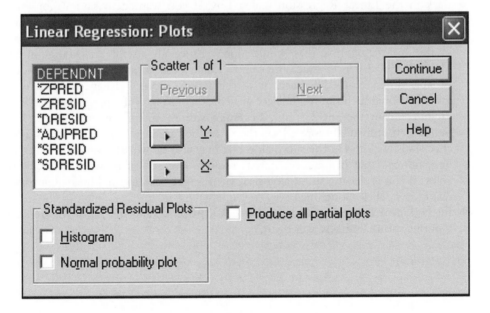

In this Linear Regression: Plots sub-dialog box you can request a scatterplot showing the relationship between any pair of variables shown in the source box on the left. To request a scatterplot, you have to select a variable on the left by clicking it, move it to the box labelled **Y** by clicking the appropriate arrow button if you want it to appear on the vertical axis or Y-axis of the scatterplot, then select another variable and move it in the same way to the box labelled **X** so that it appears on the horizontal axis or X-axis. One of the most useful plots is ***ZRESID**, the regression standardized residual, as a function of ***ZPRED**, the regression standardized predicted value. As we mentioned earlier, residuals are observed values of the dependent variable minus the value predicted by the model, and any standardized variable is the original variable divided by its standard error so that it is expressed in units of standard deviations. A plot of these two variables serves as a check of a key assumption of multiple regression that variances of residuals are equal across the range of the predicted values of the dependent variable.

◆ Select ***ZRESID** and move it to the box labelled **Y**, and then select ***ZPRED** and move it to the box labelled **X**. To set up another scatterplot, you could click **Next** and repeat the procedure for another pair of variables. In this dialog box you could also click check boxes to select **Histogram** to produce a histogram of the standardized residuals with a normal curve superimposed on it (to check the assumption that the residuals are normally distributed), **Normal probability plot** to display a normal probability plot of the residuals, which should be a straight line if the variable is normally distributed as is also assumed by the multiple regression procedure, and **Produce all partial plots** to display scatterplots of the residuals of each independent variable on one axis against residuals of the dependent variable on the other. Unless you're a glutton for scatterplots, we suggest you ignore these additional plots and click **Continue**.

◆ Back in the Linear Regression dialog box, if you wanted to save various new variables that SPSS calculates and places in additional columns of the Data Editor, you could click **Save...**, and you could then specify what you wanted to save in the sub-dialog box that would open. Especially useful are **Mahalanobis**, Mahalanobis' distance, a measure of how much a case's value on the independent variable differs from the mean of all the scores; **Cook's** distance, which is an index of how much the residuals of all scores would alter if a particular case were excluded from the analysis; and **Leverage values**, which are estimates of how much each individual score affects the fit of the regression model. Various influence statistics listed in the sub-dialog box may also be worth saving, although we have noticed that in practice analysts seldom save any of these additional variables. If you are in the sub-dialog box, then to get back to the Linear Regression dialog box, click **Continue**.

◆ In the Linear Regression dialog box, click **Options...** and the Linear Regression: Options sub-dialog box will open.

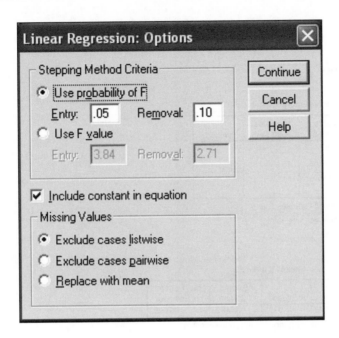

♦ In the Linear Regression: Options sub-dialog box, if you were using one of the stepwise regression methods (Stepwise, Backward, or Forward), you could set the criteria for entry and removal of variables. The defaults, which most analysts seem happy to use, are .05 probability for entry and .10 probability for removal. In this sub-dialog box you could also determine the treatment of missing values, if you had any. The default, which again is widely accepted, is listwise exclusion, which means that only those cases with valid scores on all variables are used in the analysis. Finally, you could instruct SPSS to suppress the constant term in the regression equation, producing a line through the origin, but this is seldom a good idea. We recommend that you leave the default options as they are, both in this case and generally, unless you have a good reason to choose something different. Click **Continue**.

♦ In the Linear Regression dialog box for the last time, click **OK**, and the Output Viewer will display the results of the analysis. If some of the results scroll out of sight, use the scroll bars as explained in section 2.5. To print a hard copy of the output, follow the procedure described in section 3.2. To print a selection of the output, first click or shift-click the desired names in the panel on the left, or click the tables themselves, then use the procedure described in section 3.3.

12.4 RESULTS

Regression

Variables Entered/Removed[b]

Model	Variables Entered	Variables Removed	Method
1	grants, abrc, pubs, staffing, articles[a]	.	Enter

a. All requested variables entered.

b. Dependent Variable: rating

Model Summary[b]

Model	R	R Square	Adjusted R Square	Std. Error of the Estimate
1	.794[a]	.631	.463	.85445

a. Predictors: (Constant), grants, abrc, pubs, staffing, articles

b. Dependent Variable: rating

ANOVA[b]

Model		Sum of Squares	df	Mean Square	F	Sig.
1	Regression	13.734	5	2.747	3.762	.031[a]
	Residual	8.031	11	.730		
	Total	21.765	16			

a. Predictors: (Constant), grants, abrc, pubs, staffing, articles

b. Dependent Variable: rating

Coefficients[a]

Model		Unstandardized Coefficients		Standardized Coefficients	t	Sig.
		B	Std. Error	Beta		
1	(Constant)	2.140	.604		3.540	.005
	staffing	.121	.038	.788	3.211	.008
	pubs	.049	.060	.229	.808	.436
	articles	-.160	.355	-.143	-.451	.661
	abrc	9.80E-006	.000	.055	.223	.828
	grants	-3.3E-005	.000	-.280	-1.323	.213

a. Dependent Variable: rating

Residuals Statisticsᵃ

	Minimum	Maximum	Mean	Std. Deviation	N
Predicted Value	2.7899	5.7887	3.8824	.92648	17
Residual	-1.79187	1.08824	.00000	.70847	17
Std. Predicted Value	-1.179	2.058	.000	1.000	17
Std. Residual	-2.097	1.274	.000	.829	17

a. Dependent Variable: rating

Scatterplot

Dependent Variable: rating

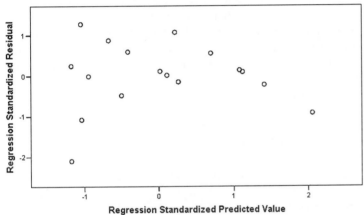

The first table of the output, headed **Variables Entered/Removed**, confirms that all five of the independent or predictor variables were entered and none were removed, because you used the standard multiple regression technique and not a stepwise procedure or other nonstandard procedure.

The second table, **Model Summary**, gives the value of R, also called the coefficient of multiple correlation, R^2, also called the coefficient of determination, the adjusted R^2, and the standard error of the estimate. The most important data here are the coefficient of determination, which is shown as $R^2 = .631$, and the adjusted $R^2 = .463$. The coefficient of determination R^2 is the proportion of variance in the dependent variable that is explained by the model, and it is over 63 per cent in this case. The reason for the adjusted value, which is always lower than the original R^2, is that the original is generally an overestimate, because the regression equation has been specifically tailored to fit what is usually a sample of data, and if it is applied to a new sample, it probably wouldn't fit quite as well. The adjusted $R^2 = .463$ is designed to correct for this optimistic bias. But the data used in our analysis are not sample data used to estimate population values; the anthropology departments studied were the whole population of UK anthropology departments. The unadjusted $R^2 = .631$ is therefore the right one to use in this case, and it suggests that about 63 per cent of the variance in ratings of anthropology departments in the 1992 research assessment exercise is explained by the five independent variables that we examined.

The third table, **ANOVA**, summarizes the results of an analysis of variance, showing that the ratio of the variance (mean square) explained by the regression (2.747) to the residual or unexplained variance (.730), which is an F ratio, is $F = 3.762$, and the significance of this F ratio is $p = .031$, which is less than $p = .05$ and is therefore statistically significant by conventional standards. It is reasonable to conclude from this that the results of the analysis are not due merely to chance.

The fourth table, **Coefficients**, provides data from which you can build the regression equation or model. The unstandardized B coefficients for each of the independent variables are given first, with their standard errors, and then the standardized coefficients or beta weights are given with their t values and significance levels. Starting with the intercept, marked "(Constant)" in the table of coefficients (in this case 2.14), then taking the variables in descending order of their standardized regression coefficients, which is good practice in reporting the results of multiple regression, the equation is as follows:

$$\text{RATING} = 2.14 + .79\text{STAFFING} - .28\text{GRANTS} + .23\text{PUBS} - .14\text{ARTICLES} + .05\text{ABRC}$$

Grants from sources other than research councils (GRANTS) and articles in academic journals (ARTICLES) appear at first to have had a *negative* effect on the departmental research ratings, but notice that these independent variables did not achieve a significance level of $p < .05$ according to the t test results in the right-hand columns, and so their coefficients may be attributed to chance. (If you're not sure how to interpret p values, review our explanation in section 6.4.) In fact, the only independent variable that did achieve significance is STAFFING. This means that the ratings of anthropology departments were overwhelmingly influenced by the sheer sizes of the departments. This is a well-known bias that was identified in several other subject areas of the 1992 research assessment exercise.

The fifth table, **Residual Statistics**, provides some basic information about the values of the dependent variable that were predicted by the model and about the residuals or error terms.

Finally, the scatterplot that you requested of ***ZRESID**, the regression standardized residual as a function of ***ZPRED**, the regression standardized predicted value shows no evidence that the assumption of homogeneity of variance was violated. If the values on this graph showed a clear tendency to increase or decrease systematically from left to right, then that would be evidence that the homogeneity of variance assumption was violated, although there are no precise rules for making the judgment. In that case, the results would be hard to interpret, and you would have to consider transforming the variables and then running the analysis again, but we won't venture into those deep and murky waters in this book.

◆ Click **File** in the menu bar near the top of the Output Viewer, followed by **Close**, and when a dialog box appears asking whether you want to save the contents of the Output Viewer, click **Yes** or **No**, and if **Yes**, follow the procedure in section 2.7. Back in the data entry window of the Data Editor, if you want to go straight on to the next chapter, click **File** in the menu bar and select **New**, then click **Data**. If you want to exit from SPSS, then click **File** and then **Exit**. If you have not saved the input data, a dialog box will appear asking whether you wish to do so, and you should click **Yes** and save the input data for future reference under the filename `regress.sav`.

13 Log-linear Analysis

13.1 BACKGROUND

Log-linear analysis is an advanced statistical technique for analysing categorical or frequency data. The more familiar chi-square test of association, dealt with in chapter 6, is adequate for determining whether or not two frequency or count variables – in other words, two variables measured on nominal or categorical scales – are associated with each other. Its most obvious limitation is that it is restricted to the analysis of two-way frequency or contingency tables. Frequency data are not always structured as simply as that, and data analysts sometimes need to determine whether three or more frequency variables are associated with each other. Log-linear analysis is applicable to multi-way frequency tables and is therefore a more general and comprehensive technique than the chi-square test of association. Some people find it useful to think of log-linear analysis as the frequency equivalent of multifactorial ANOVA (see chapter 10) because, like multifactorial ANOVA, it analyses the separate and combined effects of several factors on a dependent variable, which in the case of log-linear analysis is a frequency variable. Log-linear analysis is not included in the SPSS base system, so you won't be able to perform this type of analysis unless your version of SPSS includes the Advanced Models add-on option.

People who use this method of analysis without any knowledge of the underlying mathematical theory often wonder about its name – What does it have to do with logs and in what sense is it linear? This isn't difficult to explain. Like the chi-square test of association, log-linear analysis is based on the analysis of deviations of observed frequencies from expected frequencies, and in fact it uses the chi-square statistic to test these deviations for significance. In the chi-square test of association for a two-way frequency table, the expected frequency in a cell is estimated by multiplying the marginal (row and column) totals associated with that cell and then dividing the result by the total frequency in the table. When log-linear analysis is applied to a multi-way frequency table, to estimate the expected frequency in a cell, more than two marginal totals have to be multiplied together before dividing by the total frequency. To enable the analysis to be performed by powerful statistical techniques closely related to multiple regression (chapter 12), it is necessary to convert these multiplicative formulas to additive formulas. This is done by replacing the observed frequencies by their natural logarithms, because the logarithm of a product of two or more numbers is the sum of the logarithms of those numbers. Thus multiplication is replaced by addition, and the statistical model's basic equation is a linear regression equation in the logarithms of the frequencies.

For example, the prediction, under the null hypothesis, for the expected frequency in a cell of a two-way frequency table is determined by the equation

$$\ln(f_{ij}) = \mu + \lambda_{Ri} + \lambda_{Cj} + \lambda_{Ri \times Cj}.$$

In this linear regression equation in logarithms, $\ln(f_{ij})$ is the natural logarithm of the expected frequency in the ith row and the jth column, μ (lower-case Greek mu, short for *mean*) is the average of the logarithms of cell frequencies across the entire table, and λ (lower-case Greek lambda, short for *logarithm*) represents the amount by which this base value is increased or decreased for the individual and combined effects of the row, column, and interaction effects. Thus λ_{Ri} is the effect of row i, λ_{Cj} is the effect of column j, and $\lambda_{Ri \times Cj}$ is the interaction effect of the ith row and the jth column operating jointly. This basic equation can be extended straightforwardly to three-way frequency tables with rows, columns, and layers representing three categorical variables, though it becomes quite long and complicated, because it includes so many terms: μ, the independent effect of each variable, all two-way interactions, and the three-way interaction. Continuing in the same vein, the basic log-linear equation can be generalized to k-way tables having any number k of category variables.

The most popular form of analysis for multi-way frequency or contingency tables is hierarchical log-linear analysis. A hierarchical model is fitted in which, for every interaction that is included, every lower-order effect contributing to it is also included. The basic idea is simple and effective. All main effects and interactions are initially included in the model, and the table of the logarithms of observed frequencies is reproduced by estimating the log-frequency in each cell from the basic log-linear equation. It's always possible to achieve a perfect fit between observed and expected log-frequencies in such a *saturated* model. Then the effect of the highest-order interaction is eliminated, and the log-frequencies are estimated from the remaining effects. The likelihood ratio chi-square, which provides an index of the goodness of fit between observed and expected frequencies, is calculated for the saturated and the reduced model, and if the increase in its value (indicating a worse fit between observed and expected values) is statistically significant, then the analysis stops, and the conclusion is that this interaction and all lower-order interactions and main effects involving any of the same variables are significant. If the likelihood ratio chi-square does not increase significantly, then the highest-level interaction is considered nonsignificant and is eliminated from the model, then the highest-order of the remaining interactions are eliminated from the model, and the resulting increase in the likelihood ratio chi-square is tested for significance, and so on. The process of backward elimination continues until no more effects can be eliminated from the model without significantly increasing the likelihood ratio chi-square value. The effects remaining in the final model are all considered statistically significant.

Given a data set of cross-tabulated data, the only requirement for it to be suitable for log-linear analysis is that in each of its component two-way tables, none of the expected frequencies in the cells should be less than 1 and no more than 20 per cent should be less than 5. This is an adaptation of the requirement mentioned in section 6.1 in relation to chi-square tests.

An interesting and instructive example relates to alleged gender bias in graduate admissions to the University of California at Berkeley (Bickel, Hammel, & O'Connell, 1975; Freedman et al., 1991, pp. 16–19). Eugene Hammel, an associate dean at the university, spotted what appeared to him to be a bias against women in the university's graduate admissions. For simplicity and clarity, we'll show you the data from just three of the largest departments (see Table 13.1).

The figures in Table 13.1 certainly seem to indicate gender bias. It is easy to check that 49 per cent of men who applied were accepted, compared to only 31 per cent of women. Is this association between gender and acceptance statistically significant? The obvious way of answering that question is by calculating Pearson's chi-square

Table 13.1   Gender bias in graduate admissions?

	Accept	Reject
Men	526	550
Women	313	698

test of association. The result is, of course, significant: $\chi^2(1) = 69.67$, $p < .001$ (two-tailed). If you have a few minutes to spare, you might consider following the procedure described in section 6.2 to check this result. It seems to confirm gender bias in graduate admissions to the university.

But things are not quite as they seem. Selection of applicants was carried out independently by each department in the university, and it turns out, surprisingly, that there was no significant bias against women applicants in any department considered on its own. In Table 13.2 we show you the data from Table 13.1 broken down into the three departments from which those figures came.

Table 13.2   Admissions data broken down by departments

	Department A		Department B		Department C	
	Accept	Reject	Accept	Reject	Accept	Reject
Men	353	207	120	205	53	138
Women	17	8	202	391	94	299

In Department A, 63 per cent of men and 68 per cent of women were accepted, in Department B, 37 per cent of men and 34 per cent of women were accepted, and in Department C, 28 per cent of men and 24 per cent of women were accepted. In each department, the percentages of men and women accepted are within 5 percentage points of each other, and there is no obvious bias against women in any of the three.

Data such as these are conventionally analysed by performing a separate chi-square test of association on each component of the data. It is easy to determine, by performing a chi-square test of association separately on each of the departmental data sets, that the associations between gender and acceptance in the three departments are all nonsignificant. For Department A, $\chi^2(1) = .25$, $p > .05$; for Department B, $\chi^2(1) = .75$, $p > .05$; and for Department C, $\chi^2(1) = 1.00$, $p > .05$, using a two-tailed test in each case. But when the data are pooled, the percentage of men accepted was significantly higher than the percentage of women accepted, as we've seen. This is a real-life example of Simpson's paradox, named after the British mathematician Edward Hugh Simpson who discovered it (Simpson, 1951). Check these results if you wish.

But this conventional approach is unsatisfactory for at least two reasons. First, by performing repeated significance tests, we increase the probability of obtaining a significant result by chance, because 5 per cent of tests should produce significant results (at $p < .05$) by chance alone. Second, separate chi-square tests cannot uncover the significance of differences between departments or, more importantly, of interactions involving differences between departments, but these effects can all be tested by log-linear analysis, without compromising the significance level. The admissions data are suitable for log-linear analysis, because they comprise a three-way frequency table, with categorical variables gender, acceptance, and department.

13.2 DATA INPUT

The data input should be quick and simple, although because you have frequency data classified by categorical variables, you must enter the scores in a single column with grouping variables indicating the rows, columns, and layers to which the scores belong, and you must weight cases by the frequency variable.

♦ If you've restarted SPSS and the "What would you like to do?" dialog box has opened, then click the radio button beside **Type in data**, followed by **OK**.
♦ Click the **Variable View** tab at the bottom of the Data Editor, and in the **Name** column, name the first four variables **gender**, **accept**, **deptmt**, and **count**, in that order.
♦ Now define the value labels 1 and 2 of the **gender** variable. To do this, move the mouse pointer along the **gender** variable row and click inside the cell headed **Values**. Then click the grey button that appears on the right-hand side of the cell, and the Value Labels dialog box will open.

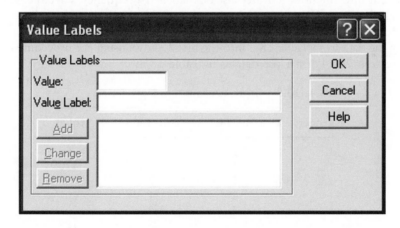

♦ Inside the text box labelled **Value**, type the numeral **1**. Click inside the text box labelled **Value Label** and type **men**. Click the **Add** button. The value label **1.00** = "men" will appear in the list box below. To define the value 2, in the text box labelled **Value**, type the numeral **2**, then click in the text box labelled **Value Label** and type **women** and click **Add**. The value label **2.00** = "women" will be added to the list box. Click the button labelled **OK**.

♦ Repeat the process to define value labels for the **accept** variable. Using the same procedure as immediately above, set **1 = accept** and **2 = reject**. Finally, define value labels for the **deptmt**: set **1 = deptmt-a**, **2 = deptmt-b**, and **3 = deptmt-c**.

♦ The fourth variable, **count**, doesn't need value labels, because its values are the dependent variable frequency scores. But, for that very reason, you do need to weight cases by this variable. Click **Data** in the menu bar near the top of the Data Editor, and choose the command **Weight Cases...** at the bottom of the drop-down menu.

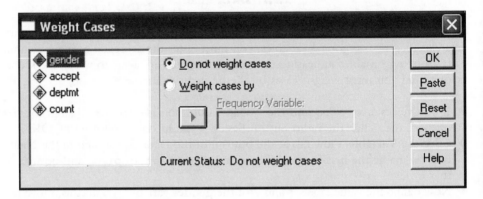

♦ In the Weight Cases dialog box that opens, click the radio button beside **Weight cases by**. Click the variable name **count**, and then click the black arrow button to move it into the now-activated list box labelled **Frequency Variable**. Click **OK**. Click the **Data View** tab at the bottom of the window, and in the data input window of the Data Editor four variables should now be labelled.

♦ Key the data from Table 13.2 into the first 12 rows using the procedure described in section 2.4. Format the data as in Table 13.3.

Table 13.3 Graduate admissions input format

gender	accept	deptmt	count
1	1	1	353
1	1	2	120
1	1	3	53
1	2	1	207
1	2	2	205
1	2	3	138
2	1	1	17
2	1	2	202
2	1	3	94
2	2	1	8
2	2	2	391
2	2	3	299

◆ Unless you've reconfigured your variables, these will appear in the Data Editor with two decimal places when you type them in (1.00 instead of 1, and so on). Save the data by following the procedure described in section 2.7. Name this data file **genbias.sav**.

13.3 ANALYSIS

To perform the following analysis, the version of SPSS that you are using has to have the SPSS Advanced Models add-on option.

◆ Click **Analyze** in the menu bar near the top of the Data Editor and select **Loglinear**.

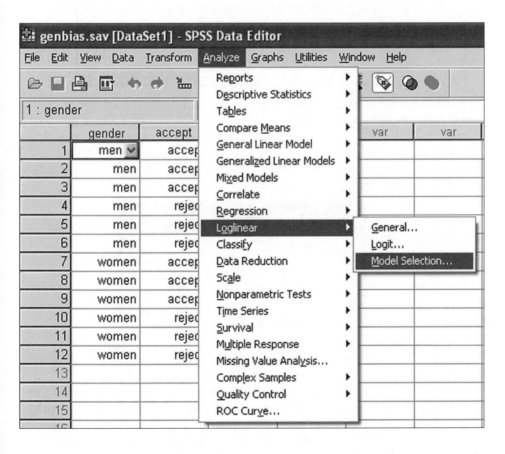

◆ Click **Model Selection...** in the submenu, and the Model Selection Loglinear Analysis dialog box will open.

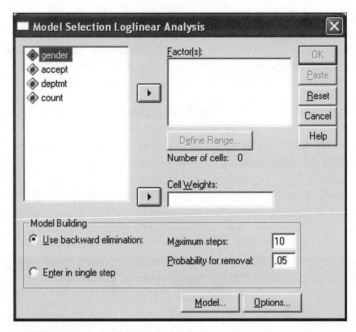

◆ Move the variable name **gender** from the source box on the left to the box on the right labelled **Factor(s)**. When it has transferred, it will appear as **gender(??)** and the **Define Range...** button will be activated. You obviously have to define the range of this categorical variable.

◆ Click the **Define Range...** button, and the Loglinear Analysis: Define Range sub-dialog box will open.

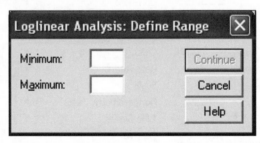

◆ In the text box opposite **Minimum** type **1**, and in the text box opposite **Maximum** type **2**. These represent the two levels of your **gender** variable, male and female. Click **Continue**.

◆ Repeat the same transferring process for the remaining grouping variables. Move the variable name **accept** to the **Factor(s)** list box, and set the range by typing **1** and **2**, and click **Continue**, then move the variable name **deptmt** and set the range by typing **1** and **3**, because this variable has three levels, and click **Continue**.

◆ Back in the Model Selection Loglinear Analysis dialog box, notice the text box labelled **Cell Weights**. You might have thought that you could weight cases by the frequency variable by moving it into this box, but it doesn't work. You've weighted cases already, so ignore this box, which is used only for custom models.

◆ The Model Building group has a radio button set by default to **Use backward elimination**. For statistical reasons, this is believed to be the best method of hierarchical log-linear analysis. You could if you wished choose instead **Enter in a single step**, but use backward elimination now.

◆ Because you've opted for the backward elimination procedure, in the text box labelled **Maximum steps** you can type a number to determine the number of steps for backward elimination. The default is 10, and most analysts use this figure, so leave it as it is. In the text box labelled **Probability for removal**, you could also change the default probability of likelihood ratio chi-square change required for eliminating variables during the backward elimination procedure. By default, a variable is eliminated if the probability of the likelihood ratio chi-square change is greater than .05, and you could, if you wished, increase this probability to make elimination of a variable easier or reduce it to make elimination harder, but leave the default in place for now.

◆ If you wished to use a custom statistical model rather than the default saturated model, which initially includes *all* main effects and interactions, you could click **Model...**, and a sub-dialog box would open enabling you to specify a custom model. If you have opened this sub-dialog box, make sure that the radio button **Saturated** is selected, and click **Continue** to get back to the Model Selection Loglinear Analysis dialog box.

◆ Click the **Options...** button, and the Loglinear Analysis: Options sub-dialog box will open.

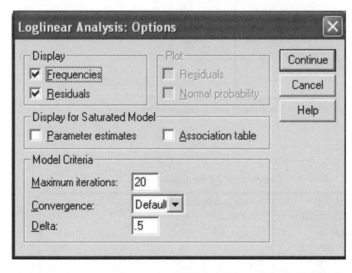

◆ In the Display group, **Frequencies** and **Residuals** are selected by default, but there is no point displaying these when using a saturated model, because the observed and expected frequencies are equal – you know what they are already – and the residuals are all zero, because a perfect fit is always achieved. Deselect both of these options by clicking their check boxes.

◆ In the Display for Saturated Model group, you could if you wished select **Parameter estimates** and **Association table** by clicking their check boxes. Parameter estimates are sometimes useful for interpreting results, and the association tables option causes the output to include tests for partial associations, which can be useful if there are only a few factors, but which produce vast amounts of obscure data in other cases. Don't select these.

◆ The Plot group is relevant only if you are analysing a custom model, rather than a fully saturated model, so ignore it. Finally, the Model Criteria group allows you to override the estimation criteria that SPSS uses in its iterative calculations. You can override **Maximum iterations**, **Convergence**, or **Delta** (a value that SPSS adds to all cell frequencies for saturated models), but there are seldom good reasons to change the default criteria, so leave them for now.

◆ Click **Continue**. Back in the Model Selection Loglinear Analysis dialog box for the last time, click **OK**, and the Output Viewer will appear with the results.

13.4 Results

Hierarchical Loglinear Analysis

Data Information

		N
Cases	Valid	12
	Out of Range[a]	0
	Missing	0
	Weighted Valid	2087
Categories	gender	2
	accept	2
	deptmt	3

a. Cases rejected because of out of range factor values.

Design 1

Convergence Information

Generating Class	gender*accept*deptmt
Number of Iterations	1
Max. Difference between Observed and Fitted Marginals	.000
Convergence Criterion	.391

Goodness-of-Fit Tests

	Chi-Square	df	Sig.
Likelihood Ratio	.000	0	.
Pearson	.000	0	.

K-Way and Higher-Order Effects

	K	df	Likelihood Ratio		Pearson		Number of Iterations
			Chi-Square	Sig.	Chi-Square	Sig.	
K-way and Higher Order Effects[a]	1	11	1134.454	.000	1006.499	.000	0
	2	7	949.660	.000	943.613	.000	2
	3	2	.784	.676	.768	.681	7
K-way Effects[b]	1	4	184.794	.000	62.885	.000	0
	2	5	948.876	.000	942.845	.000	0
	3	2	.784	.676	.768	.681	0

a. Tests that k-way and higher order effects are zero.

b. Tests that k-way effects are zero.

BACKWARD ELIMINATION STATISTICS

Step Summary

Step[b]			Effects	Chi-Square[a]	df	Sig.	Number of Iterations
0	Generating Class[c]						
			gender*accept*deptmt	.000	0	.	
	Deleted Effect	1	gender*accept*deptmt	.784	2	.676	7
1	Generating Class[c]						
			gender*accept, gender*deptmt, accept*deptmt	.784	2	.676	
	Deleted Effect	1	gender*accept	1.216	1	.270	2
		2	gender*deptmt	684.106	2	.000	2
		3	accept*deptmt	125.507	2	.000	2
2	Generating Class[c]						
			gender*deptmt, accept*deptmt	2.000	3	.572	
	Deleted Effect	1	gender*deptmt	753.130	2	.000	2
		2	accept*deptmt	194.531	2	.000	2
3	Generating Class[c]						
			gender*deptmt, accept*deptmt	2.000	3	.572	

a. For 'Deleted Effect', this is the change in the Chi-Square after the effect is deleted from the model.

b. At each step, the effect with the largest significance level for the Likelihood Ratio Change is deleted, provided the significance level is larger than .050.

c. Statistics are displayed for the best model at each step after step 0.

Convergence Information[a]

Generating Class	gender*deptmt, accept*deptmt	
Number of Iterations		0
Max. Difference between Observed and Fitted Marginals		.000
Convergence Criterion		.391

a. Statistics for the final model after Backward Elimination.

Goodness-of-Fit Tests

	Chi-Square	df	Sig.
Likelihood Ratio	2.000	3	.572
Pearson	2.008	3	.571

The first part of the results simply summarizes the input data, confirming the number of scores (cases) and the number of levels of each of the categorical variables. This is followed by data for the initial design, Gender × Accept × Deptmt. A perfect fit was achieved in one iteration, with zero values shown below for both the likelihood ratio and Pearson's chi-square statistics. A perfect fit is guaranteed with a saturated model, so these results are less than informative.

The tests for k-way and higher-order effects are more interesting. They tell you whether each order of effects is statistically significant in the saturated model, before the hierarchical backward elimination procedure begins. Reading the top half of the table in reverse order, beginning with the third row of figures, what these results show is, first, that the three-way (k-way) interaction Gender × Accept × Deptmt is not significant. The value of the likelihood ratio chi-square with two degrees of freedom is .784, and the corresponding probability is .676, indicating that there is no reason to reject the hypothesis that this effect is zero. This is usually written: likelihood ratio $\chi^2(2) = .78$, $p = .68$. Pearson's chi-square results are also given here, on the right of the likelihood ratio chi-square results but, in log-linear analysis, the likelihood ratio chi-square is preferred because it has additive properties that Pearson's lacks. Moving up one line to the two-way and higher interactions (the two-way interactions Gender × Accept, Gender × Deptmt, and Accept × Deptmt together with the three-way interaction Gender × Accept × Deptmt), we see that these, taken together, are statistically significant, likelihood ratio $\chi^2(7) = 949.66$, $p < .001$. Finally in the first row of this table, the one-way effects (Gender, Accept, and Deptmt), taken together with two-way and three-way effects, are also significant, $\chi^2(11) = 1134.45$, $p < .001$, but this is bound to be the case, because we already know that two-way and three-way effects, taken together, are significant – it is in this sense that the analysis is hierarchical. The bottom of the table shows the significance of the one-way effects, two-way interactions, and three-way interaction, each considered separately. The one-way effects are significant, likelihood ratio $\chi^2(4) = 184.79$, $p < .001$; the two-way interactions are significant, likelihood ratio $\chi^2(5) = 948.88$, $p < .001$; and the three-way interaction is nonsignificant, likelihood ratio $\chi^2(2) = 0.78$, $p = .66$.

The backward elimination statistics are presented next. The procedure begins at Step 0 with all main effects and interactions included, then the highest-order interaction is eliminated first, provided that its elimination does not cause a significant change in the likelihood ratio chi-square value, then each of the interactions at the next lower order is eliminated in turn, provided that its elimination does not cause a significant change in the likelihood ratio chi-square, and so on until nothing further can be eliminated without increasing the likelihood ratio chi-square significantly. This part of the output shows first, at Step 0, that elimination of the three-way interaction does not change the likelihood ratio chi-square significantly: likelihood ratio $\chi^2(2)$ change = .78, p = .68. The three-way interaction is duly eliminated, after seven iterations, and the best model at this juncture has the generating class consisting only of two-way interactions. That means that it includes the two-way effects and all lower-order effects subsumed under them – in this case the three main effects. What makes hierarchical log-linear analysis hierarchical is the requirement that when any effect is retained in the model, so are all the component lower-order effects that enter into it.

Step 1 shows that the elimination of the two-way interaction Gender × Accept does not change the likelihood ratio chi-square significantly, likelihood ratio $\chi^2(1)$ change = 1.22, p = .27, so it is eliminated after two iterations. The elimination of the two-way interaction Gender × Deptmt, on the other hand, does change the likelihood ratio chi-square significantly, likelihood ratio $\chi^2(2)$ change = 684.11, p < .001, so it is retained. The elimination of the two-way interaction Accept × Deptmt also changes the likelihood ratio chi-square significantly, likelihood ratio $\chi^2(2)$ change = 125.51, p < .001, so it too is retained. This part of the analysis shows that the best model at Step 1 has the generating class consisting of just two of the two-way interactions, namely Gender × Deptmt and Accept × Deptmt, and by implication also the lower-order main effects entering into these two interactions, which in this case is all three main effects.

At Step 2, the elimination of the two-way interaction Gender × Deptmt after two iterations changes the likelihood ratio significantly – likelihood ratio $\chi^2(2)$ change = 753.13, p < .001 – and so does the elimination of the two-way interaction Accept × Deptmt: likelihood ratio $\chi^2(2)$ change = 194.53, p < .001. Step 3 confirms that the final model has the generating class comprising both of these two-way interactions. That last parts of the output provide technical information about the convergence criteria and goodness-of-fit tests. If the goodness-of-fit test is significant (p < 0.05), then the model does not adequately fit the data, but ours is nonsignificant, showing that the model does provide an adequate fit.

What this analysis shows is that there is no significant association between gender and acceptance, and hence there is no evidence of gender bias – the Gender × Accept interaction was eliminated at Step 1. It also shows that there are significant associations between gender and department, and between acceptance and department. Looking back over Table 13.2, it is easy to calculate that the percentages of applicants who were men in the three departments were as follows: Department A, 95.73 per cent; Department B, 35.40 per cent; Department C, 32.70 per cent. We know from the log-linear analysis that these differ significantly, because the final model retains the Gender × Department interaction. The percentages of applicants who were accepted by the three departments were: Department A, 63.25 per cent; Department B, 35.08 per cent; Department C, 25.17 per cent. These also differ significantly, because the final model retains the Accept × Department interaction.

Everything is now clear. Far more men than women applied to Department A, and the percentages of applicants who were accepted by Department A was much higher than the percentages in the other departments. Although the departments have not been identified, most universities have departments that have mostly male students and are relatively easy to get into – you can probably guess what kind of discipline this was. Women far outnumbered men in applications to Departments B and C, and these departments were far harder to get into. None of the departments discriminated against women applicants. What happened was that most women applied to departments with high rejection rates. How curious!

The results might be reported something like this: "A three-way hierarchical log-linear analysis by backward elimination was carried out to determine whether any significant associations exist between applicant's gender, acceptance, and department. One-way effects were found to be significant, likelihood ratio $\chi^2(4) = 184.79$, $p < .001$; two-way effects were also found to be significant, likelihood ratio $\chi^2(5) = 948.88$, $p < .001$; and the three-way effect was not significant, likelihood ratio $\chi^2(2) = .78$, $p = .68$. The Gender × Acceptance interaction was not significant, and the generating class of the final model comprised the interactions Gender × Department and Acceptance × Department. Far more women than men applied to departments with low acceptance rates, but the results provide no evidence of a bias against women applicants in any department."

◆ Click **File** in the menu bar near the top of the Output Viewer, followed by **Close**. A dialog box will appear asking whether you want to save the contents of the Output Viewer. Click **Yes** or **No**, and if **Yes**, follow the procedure in section 2.7. Back in the data entry window of the Data Editor, if you want to go straight on to the next chapter, click **File** in the menu bar and select **New**, then click **Data**. If you want to exit from SPSS, then click **File** and then **Exit**. If you have not saved the input data, a dialog box will appear asking whether you wish to do so, and you should click **Yes** and save the input data for future reference under the filename **genbias.sav**.

14 Factor Analysis

14.1 BACKGROUND

Factor analysis is a statistical technique for analysing the correlations between a number of variables in order to reduce them to a smaller number of underlying dimensions, called *factors*, and to determine the correlation of each of the original variables with each factor. Francis Galton and Karl Pearson laid the groundwork with their work on correlation (see chapter 5), and the English statistician and psychologist Charles Spearman (1904) developed the earliest version of factor analysis. In his seminal article, Spearman used the technique to show that all forms of mental activity have a fundamental factor in common that he named g (for general factor) and interpreted as mental energy. Nowadays, it is called general intelligence.

The basic assumption underlying factor analysis is that correlations between many variables can sometimes be explained by a relatively small number of underlying factors. Factor analysis starts with complex and obscure input data and, if all goes well, produces simple and easily interpretable output. It normally proceeds through three steps. First, a correlation matrix of the original variables is computed; second, a few factors are extracted from the correlation matrix; and third, the factors are rotated to maximize the correlation of each variable with one of the factors.

The example that you'll analyse was published by the US psychologist Louis Leon Thurstone (1947, pp. 117–124) in an influential book on factor analysis. It's different from most of the computational examples in this book inasmuch as it involves physical rather than social or psychological data, but for that very reason it's highly illuminating. It will give you an intuitive understanding of what factor analysis actually achieves. To minimize the tedium of data input, we've selected only a portion of Thurstone's data set and, as it turns out, this hardly affects the results. The data are measurements taken from 18 cylinders. The diameters of the cylinders were 1 inch, 2 inches, or 3 inches, their lengths were 2 inches, 3 inches, or 4 inches, and their specific gravities (the ratios of their densities to the density of water) were 1 or 2. Table 14.1 shows the diameters, lengths, and specific gravities of the 18 cylinders.

Thurstone proceeded to calculate several values for each cylinder, all but one of them based on the diameter or the diameter and length measurements, and the remaining one based on diameter, length, and specific gravity. This resulted in seven

Table 14.1 The diameter (d), length (l), and specific gravity (s) of 18 cylinders

Cylinder	d	l	s	Cylinder	d	l	s
1	1	2	1	10	1	2	2
2	2	2	1	11	2	2	2
3	3	2	1	12	3	2	2
4	1	3	1	13	1	3	2
5	2	3	1	14	2	3	2
6	3	3	1	15	3	3	2
7	1	4	1	16	1	4	2
8	2	4	1	17	2	4	2
9	3	4	1	18	3	4	2

variables that he used in his factor analysis and that you will analyse again. The seven variables are diameter (d), length (l), base area ($\pi d^2/4$), side area (πdl), volume ($\pi d^2 l/4$), diagonal ($\sqrt{[d^2 + l^2]}$), and weight (specific gravity × volume). These seven variables are displayed in Table 14.2, in the format in which you will be keying them into the Data Editor.

We know exactly what these variables represent, and we also know that the first two, diameter and length, explain virtually all others, apart from the weight variable, which is explained partly by diameter and length but also by its own special factor, specific gravity, that doesn't come in to any of the others. But suppose we didn't know what the variables were. Could we recover the underlying factors through factor analysis?

14.2 DATA INPUT

The scores shown in Table 14.2 are about as small a data set as one can reasonably use for meaningful factor analysis. There are no fixed rules for the number of scores required, but correlation coefficients tend to be unreliable when estimated from small samples, and small samples are therefore unlikely to yield satisfactory results, especially when the correlations between variables are small. Some authorities recommend a minimum of five times as many cases (rows) as variables (columns). It is certainly essential to have more cases than variables. Thurstone's cylinder data yield strong,

Table 14.2   Seven variables from measurements of 18 cylinders

diameter	length	basearea	sidearea	volume	diagonal	weight
1	2	.79	6.28	1.57	2.24	1.57
2	2	3.14	12.57	6.28	2.83	6.28
3	2	7.07	18.85	14.14	3.61	14.14
1	3	.79	9.42	2.36	3.16	2.36
2	3	3.14	18.85	9.42	3.61	9.42
3	3	7.07	28.27	21.21	4.24	21.21
1	4	.79	12.57	3.14	4.12	3.14
2	4	3.14	25.13	12.57	4.47	12.57
3	4	7.07	37.70	28.27	5.00	28.27
1	2	.79	6.28	1.57	2.24	3.14
2	2	3.14	12.57	6.28	2.83	12.57
3	2	7.07	18.85	14.14	3.61	28.27
1	3	.79	9.42	2.36	3.16	4.71
2	3	3.14	18.85	9.42	3.61	18.85
3	3	7.07	28.27	21.21	4.24	42.41
1	4	.79	12.57	3.14	4.12	6.28
2	4	3.14	25.13	12.57	4.47	25.13
3	4	7.07	37.70	28.27	5.00	56.55

reliable correlations, and there are more cases (cylinders) than variables, so the factor analysis should work. Keying the data in will not take you more than a few minutes.

◆ If you've restarted SPSS and the "What would you like to do?" dialog box has opened, then click the radio button beside **Type in data**, followed by **OK**.

◆ Click the **Variable View** tab at the bottom of the Data Editor, and in the **Name** column, name the first seven variables, in order, `diameter`, `length`, `basearea`, `sidearea`, `volume`, `diagonal`, and `weight`. These variables are all scores, and none of them needs category labels.

◆ Click the **Data View** tab at the bottom of the window, and in the data input window of the Data Editor seven variables should now be labelled. Key the data from Table 14.2 into the first 18 rows using the procedure described in section 2.4. Save the input data for future reference under the filename `factors.sav`.

14.3 ANALYSIS

Factor analysis uses heavy-duty matrix algebra to perform its calculations, but from your point of view the analysis will not be too difficult.

◆ Click **Analyze** in the menu bar near the top of the Data Editor and select **Data Reduction**.

◆ Click **Factor...**, and the main Factor Analysis dialog box will open.

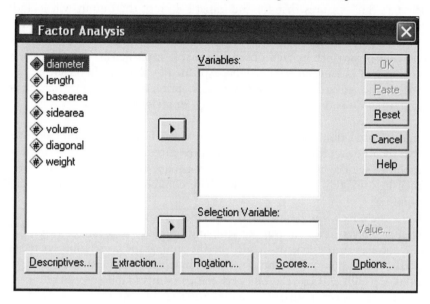

◆ Move all seven variables from the source box on the left to the **Variables** box on the right. You can select all of them at once by making sure that the first variable name is highlighted (click it if it isn't) and then holding down the shift key and clicking the last variable. When all seven variables are selected (highlighted), click the black arrow button to move them to the **Variables** box.

◆ Ignore the **Selection Variable** text box. A selection variable is a grouping variable that is used to restrict analysis to a selection of the data in the Data Editor. You are using all the data, and you haven't included a selection variable for picking out cases.

◆ Click the **Descriptives...** button, and the Factor Analysis: Descriptives sub-dialog box will open.

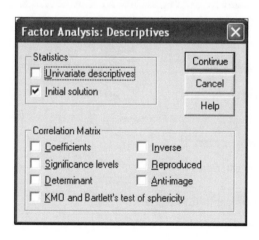

In the Statistics group, **Initial solution** is selected by default, and you should not deselect it. This ensures that for the initial solution, the output will include communalities (the proportion of the variance in each variable accounted for by the factors that the variable has in common with other variables), eigenvalues (estimates of the proportion of variance in each observed variable explained by each factor), and the percentages of variance in each variable explained by the extracted factors. You could also select the univariate descriptive statistics option by clicking in its check box, but this information is of marginal relevance, so don't select it now.

◆ In the Correlation Matrix group, click the check box beside **Coefficients** to ensure that the output includes the matrix of correlation coefficients. It is virtually always useful to see the correlation matrix. If not many correlations are larger than .30, then it is unlikely that the variables share common factors, and factor analysis is pointless.
◆ Click the check box beside **KMO and Bartlett's test of sphericity**. The KMO (Kaiser–Meyer–Olin) measure of sampling adequacy is calculated from the sum of the correlation coefficients divided by the sum of the correlation coefficients and partial correlation coefficients, and if its value is less than .50, then partial correlations are high and correlations between pairs of variables are therefore relatively unaffected by other variables, and factor analysis should not proceed. A KMO above .70 is desirable. Bartlett's test of sphericity tests the hypothesis that the correlation matrix is an identity matrix, with no correlations between variables. If the test fails to reject this hypothesis at $p < .05$, then there are insufficient intercorrelations between variables and factor analysis is futile. These are useful diagnostic tests, so make sure they are selected.
◆ You could also, if you wished, select other options to calculate the inverse of the correlation matrix and other exotica, but for now just click **Continue**.
◆ Back in the Factor Analysis dialog box, click **Extraction...**, and the Factor Analysis: Extraction sub-dialog box will open.

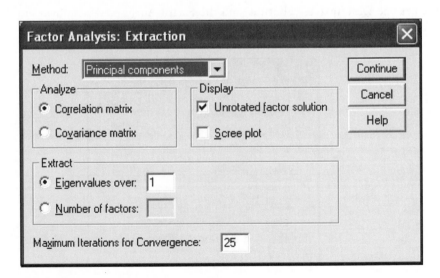

◆ The default method of extracting factors is **Principal components**, a technique that extracts uncorrelated linear combinations of variables, the first explaining the maximum amount of the variance and successively extracted factors explaining progressively less variance. This is by far the most commonly used method, so make sure that it is selected. Click the arrow on the right of the list box and select it from the drop-down list if it is not already selected.

◆ In the Analyze group, make sure that **Correlation matrix** (the default) is selected. If you were to choose the alternative option by clicking the other radio button, then the factor analysis would be performed on the covariance matrix rather than the correlation matrix, but the correlation matrix should normally be used, and certainly when the variables are not all measured on the same scale.

◆ In the Display group, the **Unrotated factor solution** is selected by default. This ensures that the initial factor solution, before rotation, is displayed in addition to the rotated solution. Click the check box beside **Scree plot** in order to select it also. This will instruct SPSS to display a plot of the variance explained by each factor, in descending order from the left. It was introduced in 1966 by the English-born US psychologist Raymond Cattell, and it usually assumes the shape of the sloping mass of loose rubble, called scree, that tends to collect at the base of a cliff – hence its name. It is useful for showing the relative contributions of factors to the variance in the data.

◆ In the Extract group, **Eigenvalues over** is selected by default, and the value in the text box beside this is set at 1. This means that SPSS will extract factors only if they have eigenvalues greater than 1 and therefore explain more variance than a single variable. The alternative would be to extract a predetermined number of factors, in which case you would click the lower radio button and type a number into the accompanying text box to indicate the number. This is not usually advisable, however, so for now make sure that **Eigenvalues over 1** is selected. You should also leave the maximum number of iterations for convergence at the default value of 25 unless you have a good reason to change it. Click **Continue**.

◆ Back in the Factor Analysis dialog box, click **Rotation...**, and the Factor Analysis: Rotation sub-dialog box will open.

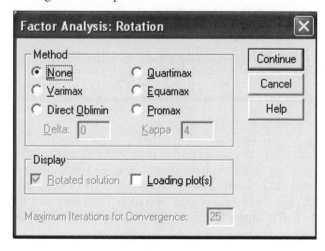

◆ Varimax (from *var*iance *max*imizing) is by far the most popular method of rotation. It maximizes the amount of variance explained by a minimum number of orthogonal (uncorrelated) variables, and this simplifies the interpretation of the results. The other methods are so seldom used that we will not even discuss them. There are so many combinations of extraction and rotation methods that some people wonder about the objectivity of the analysis, but provided that there are many variables with strong correlations among them, the results tend to be similar, especially after rotation, whatever extraction and rotation methods are used. Click the radio button beside **Varimax** to select it.

◆ In the Display group, **Rotated solution** will automatically be selected, with a tick appearing in its check box, so that the results of the rotated solution will be displayed. You could, if you wished, also request loading plots, showing the results graphically, but for now just click **Continue**.

◆ Back again in the Factor Analysis dialog box, you could if you wished click **Scores...** to open a sub-dialog box in which you could save factor scores as variables, but these are seldom useful. If you have opened the Factor Analysis: Factor Scores sub-dialog box, then click **Continue**. In the main Factor Analysis dialog box, click **Options...**, and the Factor Analysis: Options sub-dialog box will open.

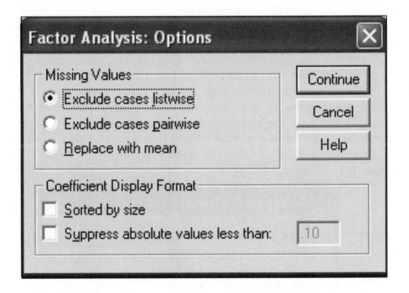

◆ Here, you could change the system default for handling missing values, which is to exclude cases listwise – that is, to exclude every case that has missing values on any variable – but the default is usually best, and you don't have any missing data. However, it is worth doing something in the Coefficient Display Format group. Click the check box beside **Sorted by size** to make the output list the factors with high loadings first, and click the check box beside **Suppress absolute**

values less than **.10** (leave the default value at .10 when it is activated) so that the output omits tiny factor loadings. These two selections will make the output easier to read. Click **Continue**.

◆ Back in the main Factor Analysis dialog box for the last time, click **OK**, and the Output Viewer will appear with the results of the factor analysis.

14.4 RESULTS

Factor Analysis

Correlation Matrix

		diameter	length	basearea	sidearea	volume	diagonal	weight
Corre lation	diameter	1.000	.000	.990	.812	.895	.557	.787
	length	.000	1.000	.000	.541	.348	.822	.306
	basearea	.990	.000	1.000	.803	.905	.559	.796
	sidearea	.812	.541	.803	1.000	.969	.875	.852
	volume	.895	.348	.905	.969	1.000	.768	.879
	diagonal	.557	.822	.559	.875	.768	1.000	.675
	weight	.787	.306	.796	.852	.879	.675	1.000

KMO and Bartlett's Test

Kaiser-Meyer-Olkin Measure of Sampling Adequacy.		.645
Bartlett's Test of Sphericity	Approx. Chi-Square	309.454
	df	21
	Sig.	.000

Communalities

	Initial	Extraction
diameter	1.000	.971
length	1.000	1.000
basearea	1.000	.976
sidearea	1.000	.974
volume	1.000	.972
diagonal	1.000	.967
weight	1.000	.823

Extraction Method: Principal Component Analysis.

Total Variance Explained

Component	Initial Eigenvalues			Extraction Sums of Squared Loadings			Rotation Sums of Squared Loadings		
	Total	% of Variance	Cumulative %	Total	% of Variance	Cumulative %	Total	% of Variance	Cumulative %
1	5.217	74.524	74.524	5.217	74.524	74.524	4.411	63.013	63.013
2	1.467	20.954	95.478	1.467	20.954	95.478	2.273	32.465	95.478
3	.222	3.168	98.646						
4	.076	1.088	99.734						
5	.018	.258	99.991						
6	.000	.005	99.997						
7	.000	.003	100.000						

Extraction Method: Principal Component Analysis.

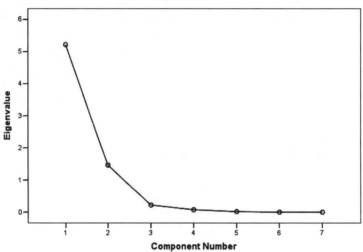

Scree Plot

Component Matrix[a]

	Component	
	1	2
volume	.982	
sidearea	.979	.126
weight	.903	
basearea	.887	-.433
diameter	.886	-.432
diagonal	.846	.501
length	.437	.899

Extraction Method: Principal Component Analysis.

a. 2 components extracted.

154

Rotated Component Matrix[a]

	Component	
	1	2
basearea	.987	
diameter	.985	
volume	.912	.375
weight	.843	.336
sidearea	.809	.565
length		.999
diagonal	.518	.836

Extraction Method: Principal Component Analysis.
Rotation Method: Varimax with Kaiser Normalization.
 a. Rotation converged in 3 iterations.

Component Transformation Matrix

Component	1	2
1	.886	.464
2	-.464	.886

Extraction Method: Principal Component Analysis.
Rotation Method: Varimax with Kaiser Normalization.

The correlation matrix is displayed first. Because of the unusual nature of the data, the correlations are generally high, and only a few of them are below .30, so it's reasonable to proceed with factor analysis.

The second table displays the results of the KMO (Kaiser–Meyer–Olin) measure of sampling adequacy and Bartlett's test of sphericity. The KMO value is above .50, which means that factor analysis can proceed, and Bartlett's test rejects the hypothesis (at $p < .001$) that the correlation matrix is an identity matrix, without significant correlations between variables, which confirms that the data are suitable for factor analysis. The diagnostic tests have all produced satisfactory results.

The next item of output is a table of communalities, showing how much of the variance in the original variables is explained by the factors that have been extracted. For the initial factors, all the variance is explained, as is always the case with principal components factor analysis. The second column gives the results after the final factor extraction. You can see that 97.1 per cent of the variance in diameter and 100 per cent of the variance in length has been explained by the extracted factors, and so on. The lowest figure is for the weight factor, only 82.3 per cent of its variance having been explained.

The table headed **Total Variance Explained** shows all the factors extracted, in descending order of their eigenvalues, together with the percentage of the variance in the original variables explained by each factor, and the cumulative percentage of variance explained after the extraction of factors with progressively lower eigenvalues.

The columns on the right of the table show the sums of squared factor loadings before and after rotation, with the total, percentage of variance, and cumulative percentage of variance indicated in each case. What is clear from this table is that the first extracted factor explains 74.52 per cent of the variance in the original variables, the second explains a further 20.95 per cent, and the other factors each explain only tiny amounts of the variance and are not retained in the analysis.

The Scree plot, shown next in the output, confirms this. The first two factors account for most of the variance, and from the third extracted factor onwards, hardly any more variance is explained.

The final three tables contain the most important results. The **Component Matrix** shows that two components or factors were extracted and lists the factor loadings before rotation, and the **Rotated Component Matrix** shows the same results after rotation. The **Component Transformation Matrix** merely records the matrix algebra of rotation: the unrotated matrix was multiplied by the component transformation matrix to produce the rotated matrix. The component matrices, also called factor matrices, are the important ones. They show the two extracted factors, represented by columns, and the figures inside them are the factor loadings for each of the original variables. Factor loadings are correlations of the original variables with each of the extracted factors. The reason why some factor loadings (correlations) are missing from these tables is that you instructed SPSS to suppress absolute values less than .10 to make the tables easier to read.

Varimax rotation, which you selected, maximizes the amount of variance explained by a minimum number of variables and, as you can see, it has the effect of clarifying the results. In the rotated component or factor matrix, base area and diameter correlate very highly with Factor 1, and length correlates almost perfectly with Factor 2. If you knew nothing about the nature of the seven original variables, except that they are all measures taken from cylinders, you could conclude from an examination of the rotated component or factor matrix that two underlying factors suffice to explain all the variables, to a high degree for the first six variables and to a lesser degree for the seventh. You would also know that the first factor is highly correlated with the first two variables and that the second is virtually identical to the sixth variable. By examining these key variables more closely, you might be able to guess that Factor 1 is something like width and Factor 2 length. According to the devotees of factor analysis, we can discover the factors underlying correlation matrices in a similar way when we have little understanding of the variables. But interpretation and naming of factors are black arts, shrouded in controversy.

The usual way of reporting the results of factor analysis is something like this: "Factor analysis, using principal components extraction and varimax rotation, was performed on the data. Two factors were extracted, Factor 1 explaining 74.52 per cent of the variance in the original measures and Factor 2 explaining an additional 20.95 per cent of the variance. The first two variables were found to have extremely high factor loadings (both .98) on Factor 1, and the sixth variable an extremely high factor loading (.99) on Factor 2."

◆ Click **File** in the menu bar near the top of the Output Viewer, followed by **Close**. In the dialog box that appears asking whether you want to save the contents of the Output Viewer, click **Yes** or **No**, and if **Yes**, follow the procedure in section 2.7. You will find yourself back in the data entry window of the Data Editor. If you want to go straight on to the next chapter, click **File** in the menu bar and select **New**, then click **Data**. If you want to exit from SPSS, then click **File** and then **Exit**. If you have not saved the input data yet, a dialog box will appear asking whether you wish to do so, and you should click **Yes** and save the input data for future reference under the filename `factors.sav`.

15 Charts and Graphs

15.1 BACKGROUND

The SPSS chart function is a powerful and flexible tool that allows you to produce a wide range of graphic data summaries. Charts and graphs are produced from whatever is in the Data Editor at the time. In fact, the procedure is surprisingly quick and easy, and with a little editing it's now possible to produce figures of publishable quality, although many researchers still prefer to use Microsoft Excel for drawing graphs, especially for publication. The full range of graphics facilities available in SPSS is vast, and certainly beyond the scope of a crash course, and there are variations in the way different versions of SPSS handle charts and graphs, so we'll concentrate on just a few of the main features of the most popular graphics, namely bar charts, pie charts, simple and multiple line graphs, and scatterplots. By the time you've finished this chapter you won't know everything there is to know about charts and graphs, but you'll know more than the majority of SPSS users.

15.2 BAR CHARTS

The estimated numbers of worshippers belonging to the major religions of the world (Adherents.com, n.d.) are as shown in Table 15.1. To produce a bar chart summarizing these figures, get SPSS up and running.

Table 15.1   World religions

Religion	Worshippers (millions)
Christianity	2100
Islam	1300
Secular/Nonreligious	1100
Hinduism	900
Chinese Traditional	394
Buddhism	376
Primal-indigenous	300
African Traditional	100
Sikhism	23
Juche	19
Spiritism	15
Judaism	14
Other	27

◆ If you've just begun a new session and have restarted SPSS, and if the "What would you like to do?" dialog box has opened, then click the radio button beside **Type in data**, followed by **OK**.
◆ Click the **Variable View** tab at the bottom of the Data Editor, and in the **Name** column, name the first two variables **Religion** and **Millions**, in that order.

◆ You are going to use the first variable for the names of the various religions (the left-hand column in Table 15.1). This variable is therefore not a numerical variable and should not be defined as numeric. Move the mouse pointer along the **Religion** variable row and click inside the cell headed **Type**, then click the grey button that appears on the right of the cell. In the dialog box that opens, click the radio button beside **String**. In the text box beside **Characters**, type **20**, because the longest name has 20 characters, then click **OK** (or in the column headed "Width" change the number of characters to 20 by clicking). This procedure enables you to type the *actual names* of the religions into a column of the Data Editor where SPSS usually expects to have *numbers* entered. A string variable, also called an alphanumeric variable, can contain letters as well as numbers, and upper-case and lower-case letters are treated as distinct. The second variable, **Millions**, is numeric, so make sure, in the same column, that its type is **Numeric**.

◆ Click the **Data View** tab at the bottom of the window, and in the data input window of the Data Editor, two variables should be labelled. The first column should contain the names of the religions. The second column should contain the numbers of worshippers belonging to each of the major religions, and these numbers appear in the Data Editor with two decimal places (2100.00 instead of 2100, and so on), unless you've reconfigured this variable to zero decimal places in the Variable View window, but this makes no difference to the graphic displays. Key the data from Table 15.1 into the first 13 rows using the procedure described in section 2.4. If the column in which you're typing the names of religions is too narrow, move the mouse pointer to the right-hand edge of the grey box at the top of the column containing the variable name **Religion**, and when it turns into a double arrow with parallel lines, hold the mouse button down and drag the right-hand edge of the column out to the right.

◆ Before starting to draw a graph, you need to ensure that you've entered your Measure type for each variable, which you do in the Variable View window. Click that tab now and make sure in the Measure column that you have selected **Nominal** for the **Religion** variable. Click inside the cell and use the drop-down list to change the measure type, if necessary. "Nominal" comes from the Latin word for "name", and so nominal data is the recording of names, in this example the religions' names *Christianity, Islam,* and so on. For the second variable **Millions**, ensure that the measure type is set to **Scale**, as the numbers are measured on a continuous scale beginning at zero. Setting this up at the beginning will ensure that your graphs are labelled correctly and come out the way that you intended. If your variables are not set up correctly and you start defining a chart, then you can either close the Chart Builder and alter them in the Variable View window or, in the variables list in the Chart Builder, you can change the measurement type by right-clicking the variable name and selecting the new type. This changes it temporarily for the Chart Builder but does not change the actual data set. When the data have been entered into the Data Editor and the variables correctly formatted, save the data for future reference under the file name **religion.sav** using the procedure described in section 2.7, then prepare yourself for some fun.

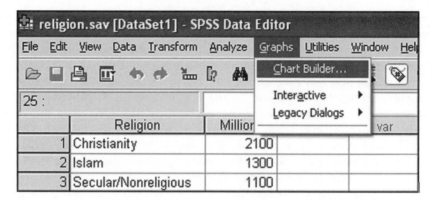

♦ From the menu bar click **Graphs** and then click **Chart Builder...**, and the Chart Builder dialog box will appear. A warning box may appear before you get to the Chart Builder, reminding you to set up the measurement type and variable labels for your data in the Variable View before you begin doing graphs (you can suppress this warning in future, if you want to). If you have set the variables properly, then click **OK**. If you're not sure, then you can either close this window and go back to check, or click **Define Variable Properties...** where a series of windows will guide you through. It will not examine string variables such as your **Religion** variable, so in this case you don't need to do anything else except click **OK**.

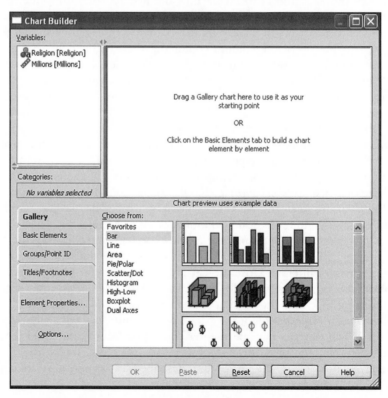

◆ The Chart Builder window should now appear. The Chart Builder allows you to see how your graph will look as you go along creating it. The **Gallery** tab allows you to look at example charts to the right of the screen and pick the one that you want. Click down the options on the **Choose from:** list and have a look at the types of graphs that are available. From this Chart Builder you can create bar charts, line charts, pie charts, scatterplots, and so on. We're going to start with a bar chart, so click **Bar** and look at the top row of the examples that appear. There's a simple bar chart on the top left, a clustered bar chart, and a stacked bar chart on the right – you can see what they're called by holding the mouse pointer over them. These are also available as 3-D versions. Click and drag the **Simple Bar** in the top row to the large white preview pane above it. As you do this, you'll notice that another dialog box called Element Properties has opened up – we'll come to it in a minute. The bar chart that initially appears is not based on your data; it's just an example of the type of chart you're creating.

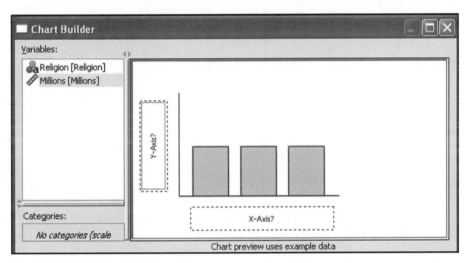

◆ Now you need to specify what the X- and Y-axes contain. The two dashed boxes are called *drop zones*. Click **Religion** in the **Variables** list and drag it to the **X-Axis** drop zone and release it there. Do the same for **Millions**, but drag it to the **Y-Axis** drop zone.

◆ The Element Properties dialog box usually opens on the right-hand side of the screen (sometimes the left in SPSS 16), but can be moved using drag and drop if you want. In the Element Properties dialog box, you now need to specify what you want the X- and Y-axes and bars to represent. First click Bar1 at the top of the **Edit Properties of:** list. Below it, you'll see a drop-down menu labelled **Statistics**, in which you can select what the bars represent by clicking the arrow on the right. In this example, we have typed the total number of worshippers in the data set, so click the little arrow on the right and, scrolIng up or down the list if necessary, change the statistic from the default of **Mean** so that it shows **Value** (the actual value that you typed in). Click **Apply**. If you try to leave a dialog box without applying the changes, you'll be prompted to remind you to apply them.

◆ If you had raw data in a large data set, then you could tell SPSS to compute the Mean, Sum, Minimum, Maximum, Mode, or other options by picking whatever you wanted from this drop-down menu to show what the bars represent. If you had raw data and selected an option such as **Mean**, then (in SPSS 15 and 16) you could also ask for error bars to be displayed, by putting a tick the **Display error bars** check box and then selecting the details of the error bars that you wanted. At the bottom of this box is an option to change the style of the bar, but we'll leave it as a plain bar.

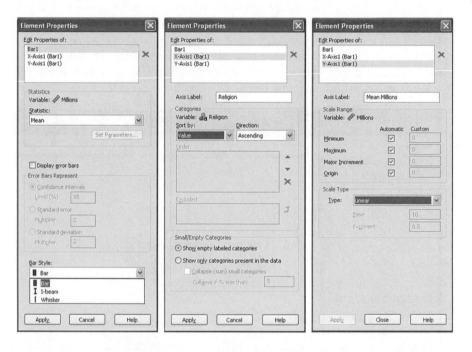

◆ Next, still in the Element Properties dialog box, click **X-Axis (Bar1)** in the **Edit Properties of:** list and new options will appear underneath. You are now formatting the X-axis of your graph. If you wanted to change the Axis Label then you could type a new label into the Axis Label box (SPSS 15 and 16), but the one we've got is fine. Below that you have options of how you want the X-axis categories displayed. You can choose to sort them by Label or Value. If you sort them ascending by Label, then your graph will have the religions displayed with names at the start of the alphabet on the left and ones at the end of the alphabet on the right. If you sort them by values, then (surprisingly) the largest number of worshippers will be on the left if you pick ascending, or on the right if you pick descending, and the rest will be sorted in size. In this example, let's click **Value** and **Ascending**. Click **Apply** (if you haven't changed anything, the button will be greyed out and you needn't click it).

◆ Finally, still in the Element Properties dialog box, click **Y-Axis (Bar1)** in the **Edit Properties of:** list and new options will appear underneath. You are now formatting the Y-axis of your graph. If you wanted to change the Axis Label, then you could type a new label into the Axis Label box (SPSS 15 and 16), but the one we've got is fine. Beneath this is the **Scale Range** box where you can format the Y-axis scale. The minimum and maximum values of the scale are automatically calculated from your data and the increment is automatically generated too, but if you wanted to customize these values you could untick the **Automatic** box and type in your own custom values. For our example, the automatic values are fine, so just click **Apply** (unless it's greyed out) and then **Close**. If, at any time, you want the Element Properties box open again, then click the button on the left-hand side of the main Chart Builder labelled **Element Properties...** (on the right-hand side in SPSS 16).

◆ The **Groups/Point ID** tab (SPSS 15 and 16) has options that you don't need in this example but are useful to know about. The **Panel** variables allow you to split a graph into two or more separate ones with the same axes, split by a categorical variable such as males and females. If you were doing this, you'd tick the Rows or Columns panel check box and then drag the paneling variable (e.g., gender) from the variables list to the **Panel?** drop zone that would appear in the preview pane. We don't have a variable to split by in this example, so we will leave this for now.

◆ If you're running SPSS 15 or 16, click the **Titles/Footnotes** tab to add up to two titles, a subtitle, and two footnotes. This is available in SPSS 14 under an **Optional Elements** tab. Once you select one of these, and in SPSS 14 drag it to your preview pane, it will appear in the list at the top of the **Element Properties** box, from where (if you click it) you can edit the title/footnote by typing in the **Content:** box beneath it. For now, click **Title 1** and then in the **Content** text box in the Element Properties dialog box type **Table 1 World Religions**. Click **Apply** and then **Close**.

◆ Back in the Chart Builder, click **OK**, and the SPSS Output Viewer will appear with your bar chart displayed.

If you want to change anything on your graph in the Output Viewer, then first double-click the chart to open the Chart Editor. From there, if you first click any part of the graph and then double-click it, then you can change its properties in the Properties box that appears. For example, if you want to hide any of the categories (religions in our example), then click the bars and then double-click to see the properties box for the bars; from there you can click the Categories tab and then click the category to hide, and then click the × box on the right. Alternatively, to move bars around, you can change the order of categories by setting the **Sort by:** option to **Custom**, then clicking them and using the up and down arrows. Things such as the width of the bars, the 3-D image, and the colour can also be edited in the properties box for the bars. Double-click the chart, then play around with your graph in the Chart Editor to explore the different functions available, then close the Chart Editor by clicking the cross in its top-right corner. Resizing the graph, by selecting it and then dragging the handles to make it wider, can remove the problem of X-axis names not having enough space to display properly (or you could change their text orientation).

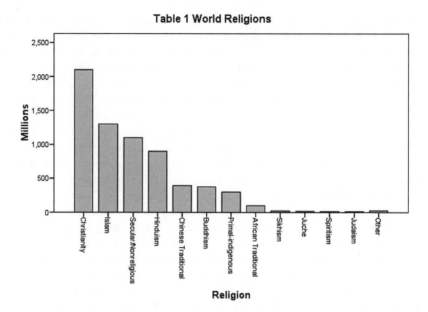

Table 1 World Religions

Religion

The bar chart shows the relative numbers of worshippers very vividly, in a way that makes a much stronger impression than the mere numbers themselves – to paraphrase a Chinese proverb, one picture is worth at least 13 numbers. This particular bar chart conveys an ego-inflating message for Christians and a humbling one for Sikhs and Jews, among others.

♦ You may save the chart by clicking **File** in the menu bar near the top of the SPSS Viewer and then **Save As...**, and the Save As dialog box will open. Alternatively, you might want to try copying and pasting the chart into a Word document, but bear in mind you cannot edit it when it's a picture in Word, so keep your SPSS output too in case you want to edit your chart and paste the updated version into Word again at a later date.
♦ Don't exit from SPSS yet, because we're going to show you how to display the same information in different ways.

15.3 PIE CHARTS

Next, you're going to display the same religion data set as a pie chart. Later on, you'll transform it into a simple line graph.

♦ To open the Chart Builder, from the menu bar click **Graphs** and then click **Chart Builder**. If you have not closed SPSS since you last used the Chart Builder and the settings from the bar chart are still shown, then click the **Reset** button. Now, in the Gallery group, click **Pie/Polar**. Click and drag the **Pie Chart** to the large white preview pane above it.
♦ Now you can see that the example pie chart is there, and you need to specify what the slices contain. The slices of the pie will obviously represent millions of

worshippers. The two dashed boxes **Slice by?** and **Angle Variable?** are the drop zones for this chart. Click **Religion** in the **Variables** list and drag it to the **Slice By?** drop zone and release it there. The **Angle Variable** changes label to say **Count**, **Percentage**, **Angle Variable?**, or **Sum**, depending on what is set in the **Statistic:** drop-down list for the **Polar-Interval1** in the **Element Properties** box. Make sure that you have set that to **Value**, as the religion data are total values in millions and not raw data that need counting or summing, and click **Apply**. Once you have done that, drag and drop the **Millions** variable on to the **Angle Variable?** drop zone.

◆ Above the **Religion** drop zone, you may notice the words **set color** or **set pattern** in blue. If you double-click the **Religion** drop zone, you can set the pie chart to show the religions in different colours or patterns, depending on which you select in the drop-down menu. For now, leave this set to the default of **color**; if you have entered this box, then click **OK** or **cancel** to leave the box.

◆ As explained in section 15.2 about creating a bar chart, we now need to adjust the way our chart looks by using the **Element Properties** dialog box. We've already set the chart to show values in millions using the **Polar-Interval1** Statistics options. So next, look at the **Edit Properties of:** list, click **Angle-Axis1 (Polar-Interval1)**, and options relating to the slices will appear. Here you can rotate the positions of your slices by altering the position of the first slice, should you want to, but for our purposes leaving it set to the default of 12.00 (at the top of the clock) is fine, as is the setting that the slices (categories) should appear clockwise. Leave the **Display axis** box blank, as it is uncommon to show the axis on a pie chart, but this is where you would add it if you needed to. Click **Apply** if it's lit up (if you've changed anything).

◆ Finally, still in the Element Properties dialog box, look at the **Edit Properties of:** list and click **GroupColor (Polar-Interval1)**, which will bring up options relating to the legend and categories. If you wanted to alter the **Legend Label:**, then you would type the new legend into the box here (in SPSS 15 and 16), but the default variable name is fine for this example, so leave it. Beneath that you have options of how you want the religion categories displayed. You can choose to sort them by Label or Value. If you sort them ascending by Label, then your chart will have the slices going round the pie in alphabetical order. If you sort them by Values, then the slices will appear sorted by the number of worshippers in each religion, with the first slice being the largest or smallest depending on whether you pick descending or ascending for the Direction. In this example, let's select **Value** and **Ascending**. Before leaving this dialog box, just make a mental note that near the bottom of the box you can choose to show all the categories, even if they are empty (e.g., in our example, a religion that has no worshippers), or only show the categories that have valid numbers of people in them. You also have the option here of combining small categories if you want to lump them all together. We will leave it with all the categories showing. Click **Apply** (unless it's greyed out) and then **Close**. To re-open the Element Properties box at a later stage, just click the button labelled **Element Properties...** on the left-hand side of the main Chart Builder (on the right-hand side in SPSS 16).

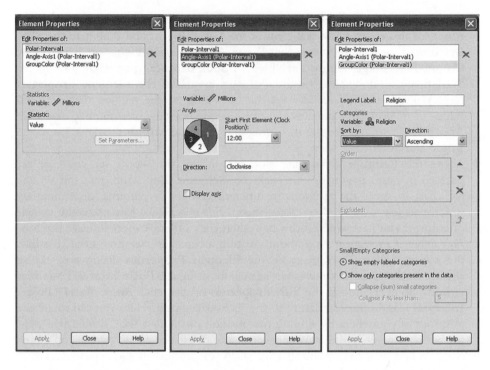

◆ Back in the Chart Builder click **OK** and the SPSS Output Viewer will appear with your pie chart displayed. If you want to change any aspect of your pie chart in the Output Viewer, then double-click it to open the Chart Editor. From there, if you click any part of the chart and then double-click it, you can change its properties in the Properties box that appears.

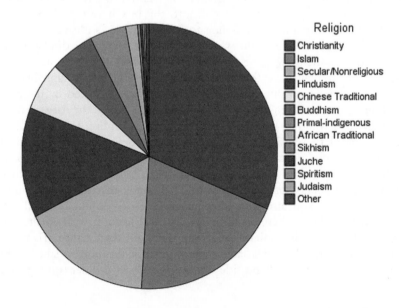

◆ You may save the chart by clicking **File** in the menu bar near the top of the SPSS Viewer and then **Save As...**, and the Save As dialog box will open. Alternatively, you might want to try copying and pasting the chart into a Word document, but bear in mind that you can't edit it when it's a picture in Word, so keep your SPSS output too in case you want to edit your chart and paste the updated version into Word again at a later date.

15.4 SIMPLE AND MULTIPLE LINE GRAPHS

You may have occasion to produce a graph with two or more lines on it to show results, especially if they include significant interactions that need to be interpreted. The procedures for creating a single/simple line graph and a multiple line graph are very similar. In fact, you can start by creating a simple line graph and then add another variable to turn it into a multiple line graph. Let's create a graph to display the data from the multifactorial ANOVA that you carried out in chapter 10.

◆ In the Data Editor (you can get back there via **Window** in the menu bar at the top of the SPSS Viewer window), click **File**, select **Open**, and click **Data** in the submenu, and the Open Data (Open File in SPSS 14) dialog box will appear. Find the data file **genaud.sav**, that you saved on your memory stick or in My Documents, click it so that its name appears in the **File name:** box, then click **Open**. The input data from the Corston and Colman (1996) experiment on gender and audience effects on a computer tracking task will appear in the Data Editor.

◆ Before starting to draw a graph, you need to ensure that you have entered your Measure type for each variable, which you should do in the Variable View window. So, in the Variable View window, make sure in the Measure column that for the **gender** and **audience** variables you have selected Nominal, and for the dependent variable **score**, ensure that the measure is set to Scale, as the numbers are measured on a continuous scale beginning at zero. Click inside the cells and use the drop-down menus that appear if necessary. Setting this up correctly at the beginning will ensure that your graphs are labelled correctly and come out the way that you intended.

◆ From the menu bar click **Graphs** and then click **Chart Builder**, and the Chart Builder dialog box will appear. Once again, a warning box may appear before you get to the Chart Builder, reminding you to properly set up the value labels and measurement type for your data in the variables view before you begin drawing graphs (you can suppress it in future if you want to). If you've set the variables up properly, then click **OK**. If you're not sure, then you can either close this window and go back to check, or click **Define Variable Properties...**, where a series of windows will guide you through setting up the value labels for your categorical variables correctly. It's much easier to set them up correctly in the first place, though.

◆ In the Chart Builder window, click the **Gallery** tab so that you can see the example charts available, and then click **Line** in the **Choose from:** list. The right-hand of the two icons displayed is labelled **Multiple Line** if you hold your mouse pointer over it. You would select it to show two (or more) lines on the graph in order to display an interaction effect, for example. But we'll show you how to create a simple line graph and then how to change it into a multiple line graph, so we'll start with the Simple Line icon instead. Drag and drop the **Simple Line** icon into the large white preview pane above it.

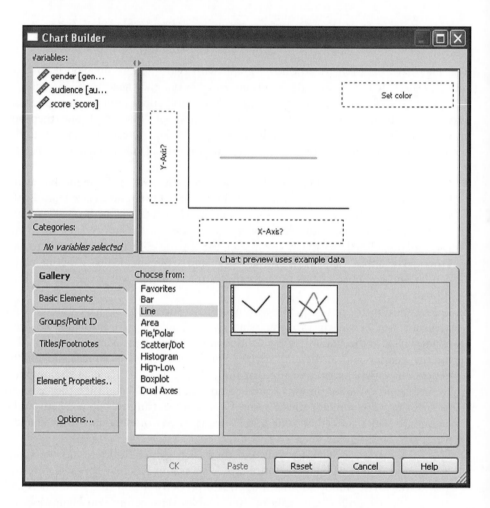

◆ By convention, the vertical axis of a graph normally represents values of the dependent variable, which in this case is **score**, so drag and drop the variable name **score** from the **Variables:** list to the **Y-Axis** drop zone on the example graph. You want the lines to represent mean scores for the various treatment conditions, so in the Element Properties window (that should have now appeared to one side of the chart builder) make sure that you select **Line1** and then **Mean** from the **Statistic:** drop-down list. If you wanted some other summary function rather than the means, such as medians or variances, you could select another function from this comprehensive list. Below this (in SPSS 15 and 16), you could choose to add error bars to your graph by placing a tick in the check box next to **Display error bars**, and then choosing what the error bars represent from the options underneath. We don't need this for our example, or the interpolation option at the bottom, so for now just click **Apply**, unless you haven't changed anything and it's still greyed out. If you try to leave a dialog box without applying the changes, you will be prompted to remind you to apply them.

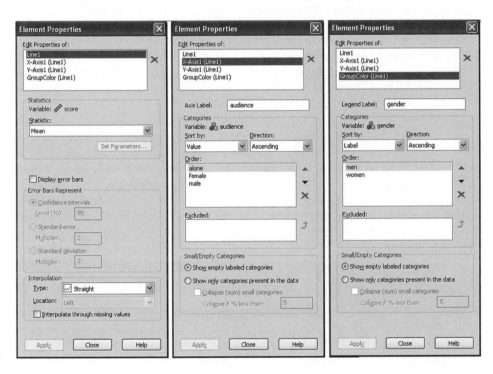

◆ Now decide which of the remaining two variables is to be the category variable represented along the horizontal X-axis, and which is to be represented by different lines on the graph. This is an easy decision, because it's generally a good idea to have as few lines as possible on a graph, so the variable with the most values should normally be the one on the X-axis. Click the variable name **audience** and drag and drop it into the drop zone labelled **X-Axis**. You have now created a simple line graph with three points on it and you could hit the **OK** button if this was all that you wanted. To show you how to change this into a multiple line graph, let's go one step further, though.

◆ If you're running SPSS 15 or 16, then find the tab labelled **Groups/Point ID** and click it. To make a multiple line graph, click to place a tick in the check box next to the label **Grouping/stacking variable**. As you do this, the chart preview pane will change to show multiple lines and a new drop zone called **Set color** will appear. Similarly, a new variable called **GroupColor (Line1)** will appear in the Element Properties box so that you can edit aspects of the lines. So, now click the variable name **gender** and drag and drop it into the drop zone labelled **Set color**. The graph should change as you do this to show you what the finished graph will look like.

◆ If you're running SPSS 14, then look for the big blue plus sign with red and blue squares next to it in the top-right corner of the preview pane. If you click this you get the drop zone for a grouping variable to be added to the graph. Drag and drop the variable **gender** into it from the source box on the left. This has the same effect as the **Grouping/stacking variable** in SPSS 15 and 16.

◆ In SPSS 14, 15, or 16, you could, of course, create a multiple line graph by dragging the multiple line graph picture icon into the preview pane at the start, rather than by creating a simple line graph and adding a further variable to it. The procedure would be very similar, and now that you are familiar with setting up variables correctly, using drop zones, and so on, you'd have no difficulty creating a multiple line graph in that way.

If you're having problems getting the graph to look as you wish, it's probable that you have not set up your variable attributes (nominal, ordinal, scale) correctly in the Variable View window. You can check the attributes of a variable in the Chart Builder by clicking the variable name and looking directly below the list of variables, where it will show you the categories for that variable, if it is categorical, or tell you that the variable is a scale. If your variables are not set up correctly, then you can either close the Chart Builder and alter them in the Variable View window or, in the Chart Builder variables list, you can change the measurement type by right-clicking the variable name and selecting the new type. This changes it temporarily for the Chart Builder but not back in the data set.

◆ Once you've got the chart looking pretty much as you intended, you can go through the different options for each aspect of the graph in the **Element Properties** window. Click the aspect that you want to edit in the list at the top, alter any of the features below and click **Apply** before moving on to the next aspect (this has been described in more detail in earlier sections about creating bar and pie charts, so we won't go through it all again here, as it is all pretty straightforward).

◆ The dialog box has a tab marked **Titles/Footnotes** (**Optional Elements** in SPSS 14) that opens a sub-dialog box in which you could, if you wished, add a title, subtitle, and footnote to your graph, as with other charts and graphs. It also has a button marked **Options...** that opens a dialog box in which you could specify the treatment of missing values, if you had any.

◆ Finally, when you have finished creating your chart click **OK**, and the SPSS Viewer will appear with your interaction graph displayed (you saw a version of this graph in section 10.4).

Graph

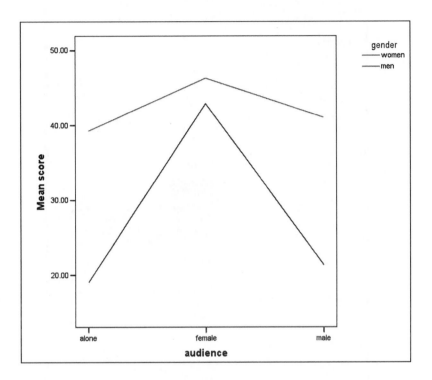

◆ This chart can be edited in much the same way as the ones already discussed. Double-click the graph to transfer it to the Chart Editor. Change the label of the vertical axis from **Mean score** to **TIME ON TARGET** by clicking once on the label, click a second time to make it horizontal, and then edit it. Press return or click elsewhere in the graph to return the label to the Y-axis. Use the help menus if you get stuck at any time.
◆ The lines on the graph would be hard to distinguish in black and white. This is something you can alter. Click the line you want to alter, click it again to make sure that it's the only line highlighted, then double-click it and the Properties sub-dialog box will appear.

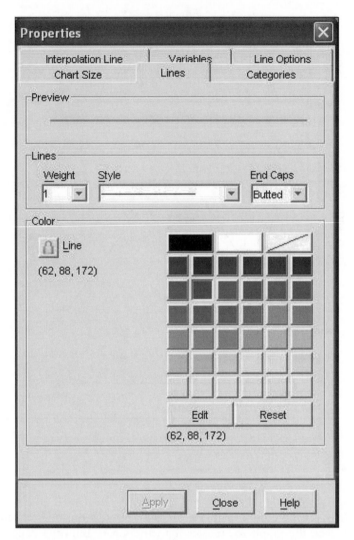

◆ Choose a weight and a style for your line, then click **Apply**, followed by **Close**. Do the same thing with the other line representing the other group, but this time select a different weight and/or style, followed by **Apply**, then **Close**.

◆ A strange feature of SPSS for Windows is that the markers – the dots, triangles, circles, or other symbols to which the lines are connected – are normally suppressed. In SPSS 14, click a line, then right-click to reveal a drop-down menu, then select **Show Line Markers** and choose the one you want from the Properties box that appears. In SPSS 15 or 16, from the Chart Editor window you can go to the menu bar and select **Elements**, then go down to select **Add Markers**. Markers will now appear on the lines. If the Properties box opens, then close it, as you need to tell it which markers to edit first. Now click one of your markers on the graph, *not* the line, or you'll only be able to edit the line properties. Initially both sets of markers may get selected with blue circles round them, and if this happens then click slowly a second time on the marker you want. Once the markers are circled, either click **Edit** and then **Properties**, or double-click. In the Properties sub-dialog box that opens click the Marker tab, then select a suitable marker type and size and choose a fill colour if you want one. You can view the changes that you make to the marker in the small Preview pane, and once you are happy with it then click the **Apply** button, and finally click **Close**. Do the same thing to the other set of markers representing the other group, but select a different style of marker, followed by **Apply**, then **Close**.

If your graph appears to freeze, or you can't get it to do what you want it to (this is not uncommon), then close the Chart Editor and re-open the graph again.

◆ Click **File** followed by **Close**, or the cross in the top tight corner of the window, and you will be back in the SPSS Output Viewer with your changed graph showing. Your graph is now ready for printing and/or saving as before (see towards the end of section 15.3). It shows very vividly (or perhaps we should say very graphic-ally) that men performed better at the computer tracking task than women, but that the female audience had a much stronger effect on the performance of women than on the performance of men, with approximately equal performance for men and women in the female audience condition. The interaction was statistically significant (see section 10.4), and the interaction graph shows what the interaction means more clearly and elegantly than the previous 56-word sentence.

◆ Click **File** in the menu bar, followed by **Close**, then **Yes** if you want to save the chart or **No** if you don't.

15.5 PANELING A CHART

In the last section, we created a graph with multiple lines on it, one showing the mean scores for men and one for women. We could, however, have created a differ-ent layout with two (or more, if we had a categorical variable with several groups) similar graphs, one for men and one for women, either one above the other (in Rows) or side by side (in Columns).

This technique is called *paneling*, and it can be used in *any* type of graph that you create with the Chart Builder. In SPSS 15 or 16, all you have to do it click the **Groups/Point ID** tab and place a tick in either the **Rows** panel variable box or the **Columns** panel variable box. If you tick both boxes, then you'll get both rows and columns and end up with four graphs rather than two, or more! This can only be done if you have two categorical variables on which you can split the data.

◆ In our example, we only have the **gender** variable left that we can panel by, so if you want to practise paneling, then create the multiple line graph (as outlined in the section above) and then, if you're running SPSS 15 or 16, click to place a tick in the box next to **Columns panel variable** in the **Groups/Point ID** tab. A new drop zone called **Panel?** appears in the preview panel at the top. Drag and drop the **gender** variable from the variable list into this new drop zone. The preview pane will now show two graphs side-by-side, one for women and one for men. If you are happy with how this looks, and have edited aspects of the graph in the Element Properties window, then click **OK** and your new charts will appear in the SPSS output viewer.

♦ In SPSS 14, with your multiple line chart (with the paneling variable included in it) in the Chart Editor (double-click it if it is in the SPSS Output Viewer), click **Edit** at the top of the window, followed by **Properties**, and the Properties dialog box will open. Click the **Variables** tab, then click and drag the **gender** variable from the **Group by:** area to one of the **Panel by** boxes beneath (panel by **Rows:** or **Columns:**). Click **Apply**, and the graph will be divided into panels.

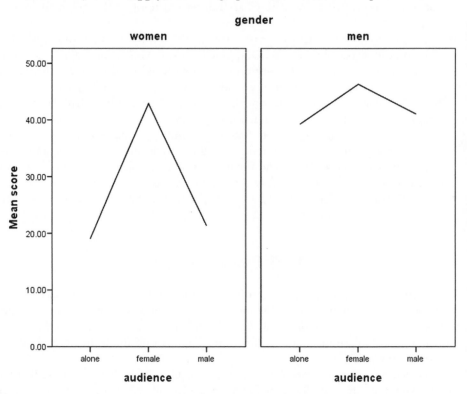

Don't forget that you can do this with bar charts, pie charts, scatterplots, or any other type of graph, and it can help you to visualize and present your data.

15.6 SCATTERPLOTS

Scatterplots, also called scattergrams or scatter diagrams, are especially useful for interpreting correlations. We'll show you how to draw one to illustrate the data that we presented in section 5.2 on the relationship between the annual number of lynchings in the southern United States from 1882 to 1930 and the value of cotton production in the corresponding years.

◆ Open the data file **lynch** in the usual way (see section 3.1). The input data from the Hovland and Sears (1940) study of lynching and cotton production will appear in the Data Editor. If you haven't created this data set in chapter 5, then enter it now or download it from the web site for this book.

◆ Click **Graphs** in the SPSS Viewer, then click **Chart Builder**. Once you are in the Chart Builder window, click the **Gallery** tab so that you can see the example charts available, and then click **Scatter/Dot** in the **Choose from:** list.

◆ Click the picture button labelled **Simple Scatter** in the top left corner (holding the mouse pointer over it reveals its name) and drag and drop it in the preview pane above. The other picture buttons are for more complex scattergrams. We're plotting two variables against each other, but if you only had only one variable, then **Summary Point** would be the one to choose.

◆ The preview pane now contains an example of the scatterplot, and hopefully by now you are familiar with the concepts of drop zones and editing the properties of the graph. Because of the convention of having the dependent variable on the vertical axis, you should put the number of lynchings on this axis. Click **lynch** on the left and drag and drop it into the **Y-Axis** drop zone, then use the same technique to move **cotton** to the **X-Axis** drop zone. Check that the statistic for Lynch in the Element Properties box is set to Value.

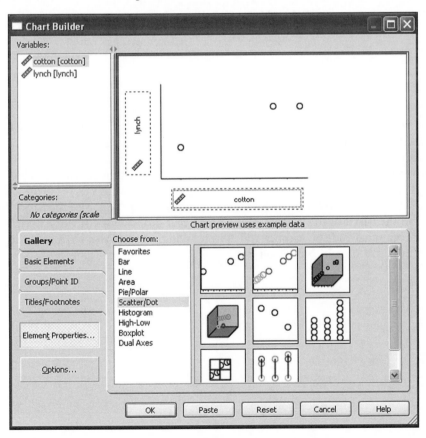

◆ Finally, when you have finished creating your chart click **OK**, and the SPSS Viewer will appear with your scatterplot displayed. This chart can be edited in much the same way as the ones already discussed by double-clicking the graph to transfer it to the Chart Editor, followed by clicking and then double-clicking any aspect you want and altering it in the Properties box that opens.

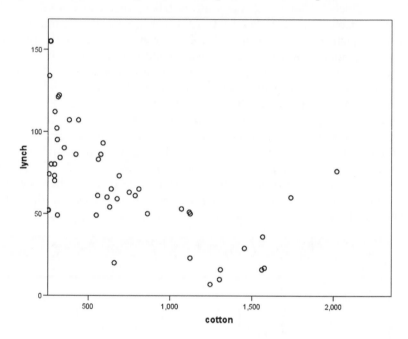

The scatterplot shows quite vividly how the number of lynchings tended to be highest in years in which the value of cotton production was lowest, and vice versa. It also shows that there were some exceptional years that did not follow this rule, despite the whopping negative correlation of −.64 between the two variables.

◆ Exit from SPSS by clicking **File** in the menu bar near the top of the SPSS Viewer, and then **Exit** at the bottom of the menu that drops down. If you have not saved the graph already, a warning will appear asking whether you want to do so. Click **Yes** if you do and **No** if you don't.

16 Handling Variables and Large Data Files

16.1 RECODING TO CREATE NEW VARIABLES

There are occasions when data need changing before they can be analysed. For example, you may have used a questionnaire that asks respondents to rate 10 statements on a scale of 1 "Strongly Disagree" through to 5 "Strongly Agree". To avoid a response bias, you may have phrased half of the items positively and half negatively, so that a person who is highly extraverted strongly agrees on half the items and strongly disagrees on the other half. Half the items will need changing before the final extraversion score is computed, and this procedure is called *recoding*. Without recoding half the items (the negatively keyed ones), the total of all 10 items would be meaningless and wouldn't distinguish the introverts from the extraverts. We need to recode these negatively keyed items so that an extravert who responds with 1 "Strongly Disagree" to them will be given a score of 5, which when added up with the scores from the positively keyed items will give a high Extraversion score. Let's use this as an example, taking these items from the IPIP web site:

Address http://ipip.ori.org/newBigFive5broadKey.htm

Big-Five Factor Markers

Factor I (Surgency or Extraversion)

10-item scale (Alpha = .87)

+ keyed   Am the life of the party.
Feel comfortable around people.
Start conversations.
Talk to a lot of different people at parties.
Don't mind being the center of attention.

− keyed   Don't talk a lot.
Keep in the background.
Have little to say.
Don't like to draw attention to myself.
Am quiet around strangers.

◆ Type names for these 10 IPIP variables into the Data Editor using the **Variable View**, calling them **ip1**, **ip2**, . . . , **ip10**. Next, click **Data View** at the bottom of the window, and in the Data View enter the data for the two participants, as shown in the screenshot (you may omit age and gender if you like).

Throughout this book we have asked you to type in data, but to save you time we have not asked you to label the data with participant numbers. When you collect your own data, however, it is good practice to enter the participant number in the first column of the data set. When you collect data from participants, you should give consecutive numbers to the questionnaires, or to the participants that you test, so that they can be identified in the SPSS file. If you have entered data by hand and made a mistake, you may need to go back to the paper copy of the questionnaire to find out the correct value of an answer, and without participant numbers on your SPSS file and on the paper questionnaires you will not be able to match up the two. So the first column of a data set is often called **Pno** or **id** or some other short name to identify it as the participant number. Do not make the mistake of thinking that the numbers in the grey area down the left-hand side of the data set are sufficient, as they only number the rows, and if you carry out a procedure such as **Sort Cases** or **Split File**, then your data will no longer be in the same order as you entered them, and these row numbers will not move with the data. Thus, you need a data column that will move with your data, and this is why you need to enter a participant number column.

EXTRAVERSION.sav - SPSS Data Editor													
File Edit View Data Transform Analyze Graphs Utilities Window Help													
5 : ip2													
	pno	age	gender	ip1	ip2	ip3	ip4	ip5	ip6	ip7	ip8	ip9	ip10
1	1	29	Male	4	5	5	4	5	1	2	3	2	1
2	2	20	Male	1	2	3	1	1	5	4	5	5	4
3													

◆ The scores on ip6, ip7, ip8, ip9, and ip10 need to be reversed so that high scores become low and low scores become high, as shown in Table 16.1.

Table 16.1 Original and recoded scores for selected IPIP items

Original	Recoded
1	5
2	4
3	3
4	2
5	1

◆ To do this from the Data Editor window, click **Transform**, then **Recode into Different Variables...** (in SPSS14 this is done as **Recode** and then from the drop-down menu **Into Different Variables...**). If you select **Recode into Same Variables...**, then your recoded data will overwrite your original variables and you will lose the original data. This is not advisable really, in case you ever want to check the original data entry or that the recoding has worked correctly, so select **Recode into Different Variables...**, which will create new variables in columns to the right of the existing ones.

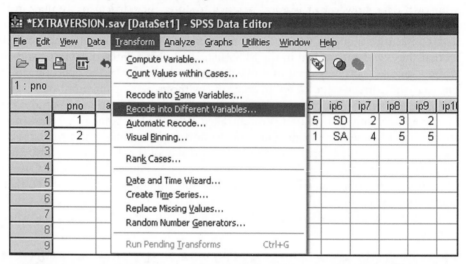

◆ In the Recode into Different Variables dialog box that appears, click ip6 in the source box and press the black arrow key to move it to the box labelled **Numeric Variable -> Output Variable** (**Input Variable -> Output Variable** in SPSS 16). Type in the new name of the recoded variable under **Name:** in this case **rip6**, and fill in the **Label:** box as **recoded ip6**. Click **Change**. You can call the new variables whatever you like, but it is sensible to make it clear that they are the recoded forms of other variables, so the simple trick of putting a letter **r** before the old variable name to create the new name is easy and clear. Repeat this for the variables ip7, ip8, ip9, and ip10, clicking each in turn to move it to the centre box and typing in new names (rip7 to rip10) and labels each time.

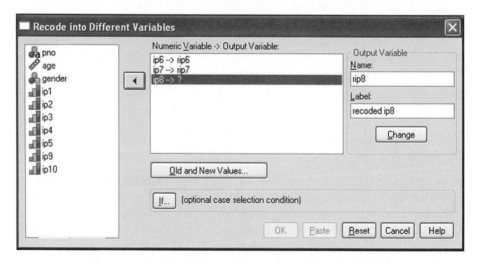

◆ Now click the button called **Old and New Values...** and a new dialog box entitled Recode into Different Variables: Old and New Values will open up where you will tell SPSS what the old scores should be converted into. If you were converting a range of scores – for example, splitting people into age categories – then you would click one of the radio buttons next to **Range** and then type in the scores where you want the cut-off points to be. In our example, though, you are just converting single scores to other scores, so click the radio button next to **Value** in the Old Value box on the left of the screen. Type in **1** for the old **Value** and **5** in the new **Value** textbox on the right of the screen. Now click **Add** and the old and new values will appear in the **Old --> New:** box on the right. Go back to the top of the box and now put **2** for the next old **Value** and then **4** in the new **Value** text box, then click **Add** again. Repeat this for all of the values in Table 16.1. You could omit 3 = 3, but since you may wish to click the buttons next to **All other values** and **System missing** and click **Add**, you should include 3 = 3 so that it is not recoded as a missing value. To exit this box click **Continue**.

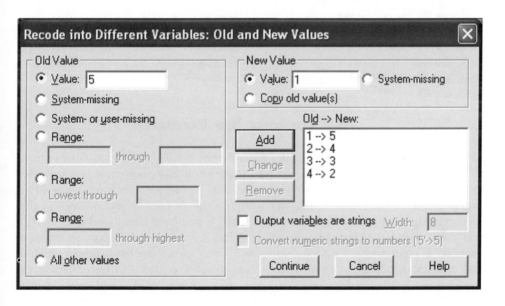

◆ Finally, back in the main Recode into Different Variables dialog box, notice that there is a button labelled **If...**, which leads you to a dialog box where you could, if needed, select which group of people to apply the transformation to. This can be useful sometimes; for example, if different groups of your participants were given different items reversed, then you would need to use this option. In our example we don't need this, so ignore the **If...** button and exit this box by clicking **OK**. Alternatively, you could click Paste to save a record of your transformations to a syntax file (if you want to do this, see chapter 17).

◆ Five new columns will then appear in your Data Editor, labelled rip6 to rip10, containing the recoded scores. This procedure works both if you have entered the data as numbers or if you have assigned value labels such as 1 "Strongly Disagree" to the variables. The new recoded variables will not have value labels attached to them though, so you would have to go into the Variable View and add them if you wanted them.

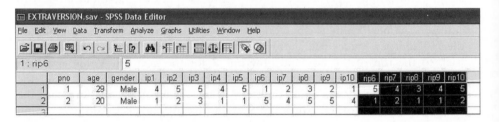

◆ If you want to exit from SPSS at this point, then click **File** in the menu bar near the top of the Output Viewer, followed by **Exit** at the bottom of the menu that drops down (see section 2.8). If you haven't already saved the data currently in the Data Editor, then another dialog box will appear inviting you to save these data, and you should click **Yes** and save them under the file name **extraversion.sav**. If you want to go straight on to the next section on creating a new variable, then do not shut SPSS yet.

16.2 COMPUTING NEW VARIABLES

Often, a researcher wants to use information from two or more variables to create a new variable that can then be put into a statistical analysis such as a *t* test. For example, the total extraversion score may need to be calculated before seeing if two groups differ in extraversion. We will compute the new extraversion score in this section as the sum of the 10 items ip1 to ip10. If you have completed section 16.1 and saved the data, then you can use the data set **extraversion.sav** for the next example. If you haven't yet done that section, then open a new Data Editor window and type in the data as outlined in section 16.1. You will also need to add on the rip6 to rip10 variables and enter the data (shown in the last screenshot in section 16.1) if you did not recode them following the steps in section 16.1.

◆ From the drop-down menu at the top click **Transform** and then **Compute Variable...** (just labelled **Compute...** in SPSS 14). In the Compute Variable dialog box that appears, type the name of the new variable that you want to compute into the top left corner box labelled **Target Variable**; in this example, call it **Extraversion**.

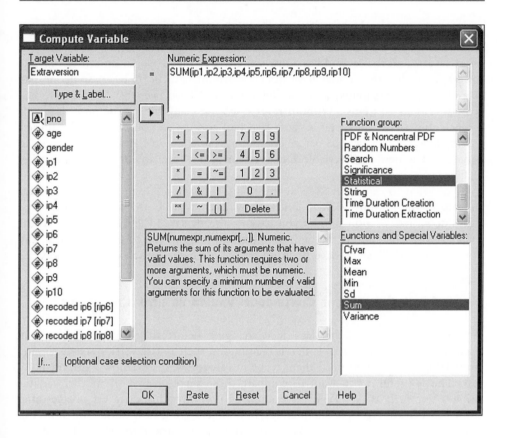

◆ In the **Numeric Expression** box at the top you must enter the formula to create the new variable. There are many different functions that you can use from the lists in the boxes on the right. Use the scroll bar to go down to **Statistical** in the **Function group** box and click it, then double-click **Sum** in the list that appears below it. The word **SUM(?,?)** now appears in the **Numeric Expression** box at the top. Select one of the ? and then click **ip1** in the variable list on the left, and then click the arrow button. Replace the second ? with **ip2** in the same way. When there are no ? left to replace, continue adding the variables with a comma between them. In this example, you should not use **ip6** to **ip10** variables, because they have not been recoded. Instead, you should use **rip6** to **rip10**, which have been recoded to allow for reverse scoring. This formula will take the sum of the 10 scores (add them up) and put the total in the new variable **Extraversion** that will appear as soon as you click **OK**.

The **Extraversion** variable appears on the far right of the variables in the Data Editor. You can see that the first participant has a high score of 44 (this person is an extravert) and the second has a low score of 15 (this person is an introvert). The lowest score that they could have obtained would have been 10 (if someone had scored 1 on all 10 items) and the highest would have been 50 (if someone had scored 5 on all 10 items). Without reverse scoring using the recode procedure, the totals would be 32 and 31 for these two participants, so you can see why reverse scoring is sometimes needed before computing a new variable and using the recoded variables. The new total variable **Extraversion** is now available for use in any other analyses you want to do.

If you want to exit from SPSS at this point, then click **File** in the menu bar near the top of the Output Viewer, followed by **Exit** at the bottom of the menu that drops down (see section 2.8). If you haven't already saved the data currently in the Data Editor, then another dialog box will appear inviting you to save these data, and you should click **Yes** and save them under the file name **extraversion.sav**.

16.3 CLASSIFYING CONTINUOUS VARIABLES INTO CATEGORIES

Another occasion when the data need changing before they can be analysed can occur when you have a variable that is continuous, such as extraversion scores ranging from 10 to 50, but you need them to be in categories, for example high, medium, low. This is useful if you want to compare those three groups on another variable using a test such as ANOVA, for example, to see if highly extravert people differ from less extravert people in their reaction times. We'll now show you how this change to categories can be quickly carried out using a procedure on the **Transform** menu. This procedure can be used to create as many groups/categories as you wish, so you could do a median split to form two categories or create as many different categories as you want.

To save you time, we'll use the existing data set that you created in Chapter 12. If you've completed section 12.2 and saved the data, then you can use the data set **regress.sav** for the next example. If you haven't yet done that section, then open a new Data Editor window and type in the data as outlined in section 12.2. We're now going to change the variable **staffing** so that we categorize the departments into large, medium, and small departments.

◆ From the drop-down menu at the top of the Data Editor in SPSS15 or 16, click **Transform**, then **Visual Binning...** (in SPSS14 **Visual Bander...**). In SPSS 14 and earlier versions this process is called "Visual Banding" rather than "Visual Binning". The dialog boxes are the same, and the procedure for computing it is the same, but the terminology has changed slightly.

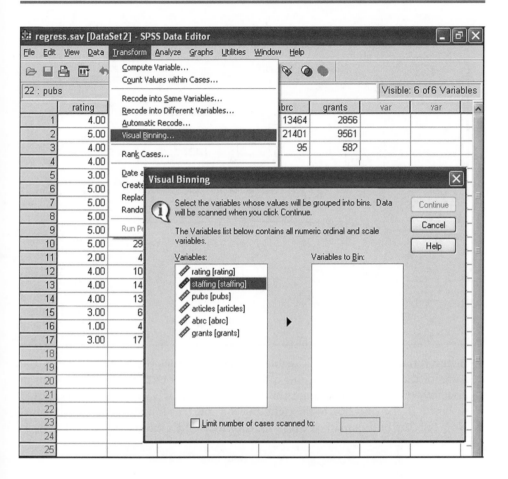

◆ In the Visual Binning (or Visual Bander) dialog box that appears, click the variable to be grouped into categories (SPSS calls this binning or banding), in this example **staffing**. Now move it to the right-hand box called **Variables to Bin** by clicking on the arrow between the two boxes. Then click **Continue**.

◆ In the next dialog box that appears, nothing will show up as active until you have selected which variable you want to use, so click now on **staffing** in the Scanned Variable List in the top left corner. A histogram of the data in that variable will now appear and the other options will become activated.

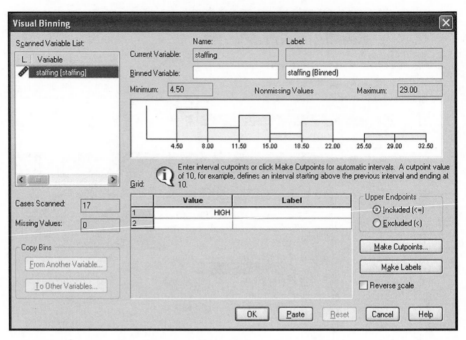

◆ In the Binned (or Banded) Variable box near the top, you need to type in the name of the new variable; in this case we will call it **staffsize**, so type this in now. If you wanted to change the label for this new variable, then you could rename it in the label box to the right, but for now let's leave it at the default name.

◆ Now click the button marked **Make Cutpoints...** and a sub-dialog box will appear.

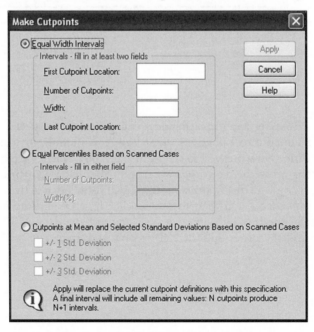

There are three different ways in which the categories can be created. First, if you know where you want the cut-off points to be between categories, then you should click the radio button at the top next to **Equal Width Intervals** and then type the value of the lowest cut-off point into the top box. Under that you would either type the number of cutpoints that there are (if you want three categories then there will be two cutpoints), *or* the size of the gap to the next cutpoint in the box marked **Width**. Once one of the two lower boxes is filled in, the other one and the **Last Cutpoint Location** values will calculate and fill themselves in automatically.

The second way to create categories is to split the variable based on the percentiles. To do a median split without knowing the cutpoints in advance, click the radio button in the middle next to **Equal Percentiles Based on Scanned Cases**. If you enter **1** into the **Number of Cutpoints** box, then the width will automatically show 50 per cent, and would give you a median split. If you enter **2** into the **Number of Cutpoints** box, then the width will automatically show 33.33 per cent, and would give you a tertile split, and to get four equal sized groups of 25 per cent each, you would type **3** into the **Number of Cutpoints** box.

The third way to create categories is to create cutpoints based on the standard deviations away from the mean. To do this, click the radio button at the bottom next to **Cutpoints at Mean and Selected Standard Deviations Based on Scanned Cases** and then click how many standard deviations away from the mean you want cutpoints at. This is a less frequently used method than the first two. We'll use the second method.

- Click the middle radio button and type **2** into the **Number of Cutpoints** box. After you click **Apply**, you will be returned to the initial dialog box where you'll see that two blue lines have appeared on your histogram, showing the points at which the data will be cut into categories.
- If you decide when looking at the lines on the histogram that they are not where you want them, then click one – it will change to red – and drag it to its new position. You may notice that the values in the table beneath the histogram alter as you do this to reflect the new cutpoint position, so keep an eye on the new number if you want to position your cutpoint precisely. Alternatively, a better way is to type the value into the value box, and the cutpoint will then move.
- Type labels into the labels boxes so that your new variable is labelled correctly. Type **Small** in the top box next to the value 10.50, then type **Medium** in the next box down and **Large** in the bottom box next to the value HIGH. Alternatively, you could click the button marked **Make Labels**, which will automatically fill in the labels with the range of scores that the category contains, but they lack descriptive labels. You could do both, adding the words *small*, *medium*, and *large* to the automatically generated labels by editing the labels boxes. Whatever you choose, try to ensure that the label accurately reflects the people in the category, and that will help you to interpret any analyses generated later with this new variable.
- Finally click **OK**, or **Paste** if you want to keep a record of your syntax (see chapter 17). If you've forgotten to give your new variable a name, you'll be

prompted with an error message to remind you. If all is well, a message will pop up saying **Binning specifications will create 1 variables**, and you should click **OK**. The original variable is still there, but a new one called **staffsize** has appeared in the last column on the right of the data set. If you want to check that your categories look correct, then do a sort on the original variable, click **Data** then **Sort Cases**, and move the **staffing** variable to the **sort by:** box, then click **OK**.

In the Data View window, you can then look at the new **staffsize** variable and compare them with the original numbers in the **staffing** variable, which has been sorted by ascending size, to make sure that your classifying procedure has worked to your satisfaction and that the labels look correct. It is always wise to visually double-check your classification using this method before going on to further analyses.

16.4 HANDLING LARGE DATA FILES

The data sets that you have worked with so far have all been small – we deliberately kept them small to save time and effort and to make it easier to see what was going on. In the real world of data analysis, you are likely to encounter much larger data sets, stretching far out of sight of the tiny Data Editor window. But one of the joys of SPSS is that big files are almost as easy to handle as small ones. Now that you know how to perform the most common data analyses on small files, you should be able to transfer your skills to large files without trouble, but it is probably a good idea to get some practice with this.

We'll now show you how to open a very large data set, the *General Social Survey* (GSS). This is a large survey, based on a representative sample of the adult population of the United States, that has been conducted annually or biennially by the National Opinion Research Center at the University of Chicago since 1972. It includes demographic data and information about social attitudes on a wide variety of issues.

◆ Click **File** in the menu bar, followed by **Open**, then **Data**. The Open File dialog box will appear. If the **Look in:** field at the top of the dialog box does not show SPSS, then navigate to the main SPSS folder in Program Files by using the arrow on the right of the **Look in:** field. Open "1991 U.S. General Social Survey.sav", either by double-clicking it, or by clicking it once so that it appears in the **File name:** field below, and then clicking **Open**. Click **Data View** tab at the bottom of the window, and you will see 1,517 rows of the Data Editor containing the GSS results for the 1991 survey. Click the **Variable View** tab, and you will see a list of 43 variables included in the data file.
◆ Let's perform a simple tabulation of sex and race – demographic variables that you might have to specify when reporting research results. Click **Analyze**, then in the drop-down menu that appears click **Descriptive Statistics**, then **Crosstabs...**, and the Crosstabs dialog box will open.

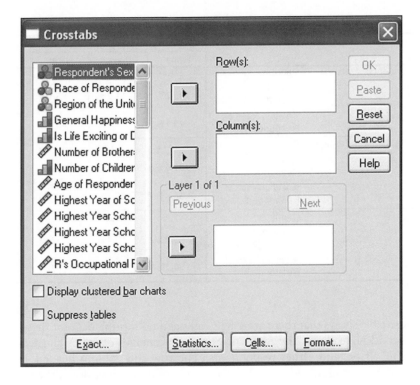

◆ In the list of variables on the left, select **Respondent's Sex [Sex]** and move it to the **Row(s):** box by clicking the upper arrow. Move **Race of Respondent [race]** to the **Column(s):** box in a similar way.

◆ Click **Cells...**, and the Crosstabs: Cell Display sub-dialog box, which we needn't show you at this stage in your *Crash Course*, will open. In the **Percentages** group, select **Row** and **Column** to calculate the relevant percentages for sex and race. Click **Continue**, then back in the main Crosstabs dialog box, click **OK**, and the results will be displayed.

Crosstabs

Case Processing Summary

	Cases					
	Valid		Missing		Total	
	N	Percent	N	Percent	N	Percent
Respondent's Sex * Race of Respondent	1517	100.0%	0	.0%	1517	100.0%

Respondent's Sex ' Race of Respondent Crosstabulation

			Race of Respondent			Total
			White	Black	Other	
Respondent's Sex	Male	Count	545	71	20	636
		% within Respondent's Sex	85.7%	11.2%	3.1%	100.0%
		% within Race of Respondent	43.1%	34.8%	40.8%	41.9%
	Female	Count	719	133	29	881
		% within Respondent's Sex	81.6%	15.1%	3.3%	100.0%
		% within Race of Respondent	56.9%	65.2%	59.2%	58.1%
Total		Count	1264	204	49	1517
		% within Respondent's Sex	83.3%	13.4%	3.2%	100.0%
		% within Race of Respondent	100.0%	100.0%	100.0%	100.0%

The first table shows that there are 1,517 cases and no missing data for these variables. The second table shows the frequencies and percentages of males and females, and of White, Black, and Other respondents. The row and column headed Total gives the main percentages, and the other rows and columns break down the percentages within categories. Among the sample, 41.9 per cent were male and 58.1 per cent female; and 83.3 per cent were White, 13.4 per cent Black, and 3.2 per cent Other.

Return to the data set in the **Variable View**, and have a look at some of the other variables. Widen the **Label** column by placing the cursor arrow on the right-hand edge of the cell in which the heading **Label** appears. When the pointer arrow turns into a double arrow with vertical parallel lines, hold the mouse button down and drag the margin out to the right. You will then be able to read the long variable labels. In the column labelled **Values**, click near the right-hand side of any cell to see the value labels associated with the variable. DK stands for "Don't Know", NAP for "Not Applicable", and NA for "No Answer".

If you have time, carry out a more ambitious cross-tabulation involving several variables. For example, you might examine sex, race, and region, entered as column variables, in relation to happy (general happiness on a three-point scale, from 1 = "very happy" to 3 = "not too happy") and life (rating of life as exciting or dull on a three-point scale from 1 = "exciting" to 3 = "dull"), entered as row variables. Play around with the various options and statistics until you feel comfortable producing tabulations of this relatively large data set. You may also use this data set to practise other statistical techniques that have been dealt with in the course.

17 Syntax Windows

17.1 BACKGROUND

Throughout this book, you've learnt how to navigate through the drop-down menus to produce the SPSS output you needed. After selecting variables and options in the dialog boxes, you clicked **OK** and the output appeared. If you're curious by nature, you may have noticed a button labelled **Paste** beneath the **OK** button and wondered what it does. Well, apart from the Data Editor window and the Output Navigator window, there's also something called the Syntax Editor, which is a basic text file. In the bad old days, SPSS users had to type their commands straight into the syntax editor, and this was complicated and tiresome. Then the GUI (Graphic User Interface) was developed, and the drop-down menus made it easier for everyone to work SPSS, as a result of which the Syntax Editor got ignored. However, syntax has many benefits and can also be easily used to impress your friends and employers! The GUI will create the commands for you, but you can keep them in a syntax file as a record of your work.

If you choose **OK** instead of **Paste**, then you'll run the command, but you won't have a record in a syntax file of what you did. So if you later find a data error in the data set, you'll have to go through all the drop-down commands again, remembering what you did previously. Having a syntax file means that the data analysis can be rerun at any time, after errors in data entry have been corrected or after more participants have been added, without the need to go through all the drop-down menus again. It also reduces the number of mistakes made, as you can check the syntax to make sure that you asked it to do the right thing, and you can make notes on the syntax file, or the printout of it, to help yourself to remember important points, such as why you chose one test rather than another one or what the output shows.

If you don't choose **Paste** but run your command immediately, you *can* see the syntax commands in the NOTES box of the Output Viewer of SPSS. This box may be hidden initially (depending on how your options are configured) but if you double-click the book symbol to the left of the NOTES heading, in the left-hand window of the Output Viewer, then it will open up on the right-hand screen. Double-click any book symbol on the left to hide/show any output that you don't/ do want to see or print. The syntax is shown in the notes box of the output file, but it is not so easy to rerun it at a later date from there (you'd have to copy and paste it into a syntax window), so we'd always recommend using **Paste** rather than **OK**.

17.2 A WORKED EXAMPLE

Let's go through an example. If you haven't done chapter 5 on Correlation Coefficients, then you will have to enter the data from Table 5.1 now into a Data Editor Window (or download the file **lynch.sav** from this book's web site).

◆ Follow the instructions in section 5.2 all the way through until you reach the Bivariate Correlations box.

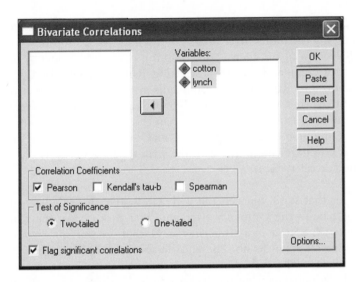

◆ Move **cotton** and **lynch** to the right-hand box using the black arrow. Click **Options** and put a tick by **Means and standard deviations** followed by **Continue**. You are now ready to run the test, so click the **Paste** button instead of the usual **OK** button that is above it. This dialog box will then close and a Syntax Editor window will appear.

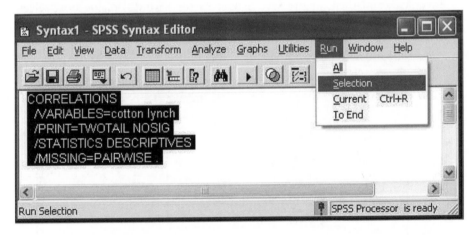

You can see that the commands for running the correlation are now in the box. Don't be put off by its appearance. The first line shows the test that you have chosen, namely CORRELATIONS. The second line tells you which VARIABLES are going to be correlated with each other, in this case **cotton** and **lynch**. On the third line the word TWOTAIL shows that you have selected a two-tailed level of significance rather than one-tailed. The fourth and final lines show anything that you asked for in the **Options** box, or the default settings if you did not go into the **Options** box. In this case, it shows that you want DESCRIPTIVE statistics and that cases should be excluded PAIRWISE if there are missing data.

♦ Select the syntax commands for the correlation in the Syntax Editor by clicking and dragging the mouse over them, and then from the drop-down menus choose **Run**, **Selection** to run them. You could run one test at a time by positioning the cursor in a command and then selecting **Run**, **Current** (or Ctrl + R) or you could choose to **Run**, **All** the commands in the Syntax Editor at once. Do bear in mind that when you run syntax, SPSS will use the active data set (the one with the green cross to the left of its name in the bottom bar of your screen). So, if you have multiple data sets open, you may get an error message in your output viewer if you have run syntax with the wrong data set selected, as SPSS will not find the correct variables.

Don't forget that until you run the commands, they haven't been done, so your results won't be in the Output Viewer until you click one of the **Run** commands. The output will appear as normal in the Output Viewer once you have run the syntax commands, there is no difference to the data input procedures or the SPSS output produced. The only difference is that you press **Paste** instead of **OK** and then run the commands from the syntax editor. By doing this you can save a lot of time later on if you want to rerun procedures, especially long ones such as computing a new variable from lots of other variables.

♦ To save your syntax file, open the Syntax Editor by clicking it in the task bar at the bottom of the window, if it isn't currently at the front, then click **File**, then **Save As...** and then, in the Save Syntax As (or Save As) dialog box, select the location where you want to save the syntax file. In this case, select the disk or memory stick, and then type the name **Lynch syntax** into the **File name** text box before clicking **Save**. Notice that the file type is a SPSS Syntax file (*.sps).

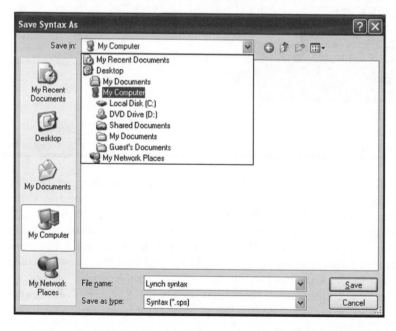

◆ SPSS syntax commands can be saved, printed, or pasted into Word, in the same way that was outlined in sections 2.6, 2.7, 3.2, 3.3, and 4.3.

◆ To close the Syntax Editor, you can either select **File**, **Close** or click the cross in the top right corner of the window.

17.3 SOME SYNTAX PROCEDURES

To open an existing syntax file, in this case **Lynch syntax**, start up SPSS and then from the Data Editor click **File**, **Open**, **Syntax...**, then click the file name in the location in which you stored it, and finally click **Open**. Alternatively, if you double-click the syntax file using your file browser window, the file will open (if you already have SPSS running). If you have any difficulty locating a file, you can try looking in the **File**, **Recently Used Files** drop-down menu in the SPSS data editor, and you should find it there if you saved it recently on that computer.

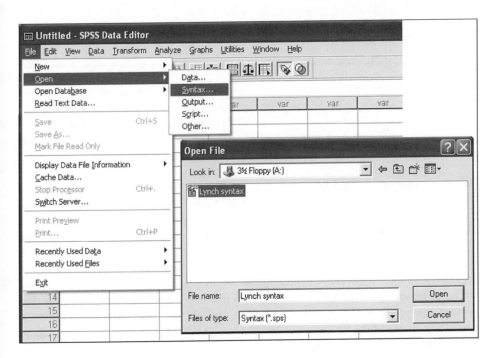

Syntax commands can be generated entirely by the GUI drop-down menus, but if you feel adventurous, you can type and edit commands in the Syntax Editor yourself. For example, you could replace the TWOTAIL command with the word ONETAIL, or change a variable name to another one to create a new correlation. Copying and pasting syntax and then editing it to put in new variable names can save a lot of time, as long as you do it carefully and get the variable names correct.

One very useful feature of the Syntax file is the facility to add comments to it, in order to document your analysis of a data set.

♦ To do this, position the cursor just before the start of the word CORRELATIONS in the syntax editor. Now either type the word **COMMENT** (in upper-case letters) or put in an asterisk (*) followed by whatever comment you want to type. End your comment with a full stop (.). For example, see the screenshot.

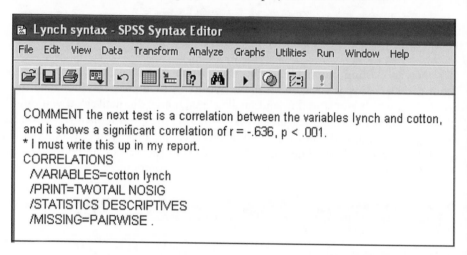

♦ If you type in comments without the word COMMENT or an asterisk, and then **Run** all the syntax, SPSS will produce an error message in the Output Viewer. In that case you will have to correct it by adding in the word COMMENT, an asterisk, or the full-stop in the syntax editor. If you don't do this, then your output will have unwanted error messages among the statistics.

One thing that you should know is that when you click **Paste**, the syntax commands will always be placed at the **end** of the syntax file. You can use **Cut** and **Paste**, though, to move the commands around in the syntax file to reorder them if you want to. It is a good idea to have only *one* syntax file open at a time, or you may lose track of where your commands are being put by the computer. As with the Data Editor, you can have several Syntax or Output Viewers open at once, but it is not a good idea to have lots open at once if you are new to using SPSS.

There are many other useful things that you can do with Syntax files that are beyond the scope of this *Crash Course*. But you should now have a basic idea of what they are and how you can use them. One of the authors of this book told the other that syntax files are a bit like dishwashers – you can get by without them, and indeed the first and second editions of this book got by without them, but once you get used to using them you don't know how you ever lived without them!

If you've reached this point in the book by working carefully through all the earlier chapters, then let us be the first to congratulate you. It would no longer be appropriate to describe you as a beginner, and you are probably already equipped to do most of the analyses that you require. You're entitled to feel quite pleased with yourself.

Appendix 1: Handling Dates

SPSS 14, 15, and 16 have a Date and Time Wizard to help users to perform tasks such as calculations of ages (or other times between dates/times). This is a very useful step forward, because dates were quite tricky previously. We'll show you how to use the wizard, and then, for users of earlier versions of SPSS, we'll show you how to handle dates by hand, without the wizard. We'll use a very small set of dates comprising just three cases that will suffice to show you how to use the procedure. Each case, representing a person, is on a separate line, and for each person two dates are listed. The first date is the date of birth, and the second is the date on which an interview took place. We'll now show you how to calculate their ages at the time of their interviews. We'll use the dates of birth (DOB) of Woody Allen (1 December 1935), Anthony Hopkins (31 December 1937), and Nicole Kidman (20 June 1967), plus an imaginary interview date for each – let's imagine that they were all interviewed on 15 February 2005.

◆ In the **Variable View** window, create two new variables by typing **DOB** and **Interviewed** in the first column under **Name**. Next to the variable **DOB** in the **Type** column, click to the right of the word **Numeric** and the **Variable Type** box will appear. Look down the list and click the radio button next to the type **Date**. A list of date formats will then appear. Click the one that suits your style of data entry for dates – in this case click **dd.mm.yyyy**, then click **OK**. Repeat this for the other date variable **Interviewed**.

◆ Now click **Data View** at the bottom of the window, and in the Data View window type in the six birth and interview dates as shown under **DOB** and **Interviewed** in the screenshot. If the dates show up as **** or are truncated, then click Variable View at the bottom of the window, and change the number in the **Columns** column in the Variable View up to 10 to make the column wider.

To calculate the differences between these pairs of dates to find out how old the celebrities were when they were interviewed, click **Transform** near the top of the Data Editor, followed by **Date and Time Wizard...** (just called **Date/Time...** in SPSS14), and the **Date and Time Wizard** will appear.

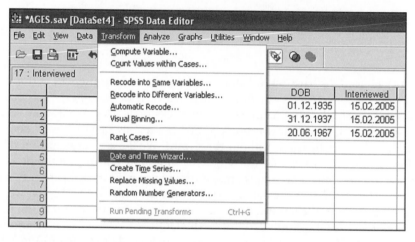

◆ In this example, click the button next to **Calculate with dates and times** and then click **Next >**. In the sub-dialog box that appears, click the button next to **Calculate the number of time units between two dates** and then click **Next >**.

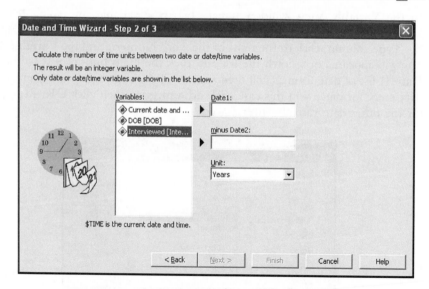

200

◆ In the next sub-dialog box, under **Variables**, there is a variable called **Current date and...** You can ignore it in this example, but you may find it useful if you did not have a variable like **Interviewed**. Since we have the variable **Interviewed**, click it, and then click the top arrow to move it into the **Date1** box. Then click **DOB** and click the bottom arrow to move it to the **minus Date2** box. If you get these variables in the wrong way around and try to subtract 2005 from 1935, you will not get sensible ages! You can change the **Unit** measurement box using the arrow, but it should automatically be on Years, and in this example, leave it on that. Finally, click **Next >** and a dialog box will appear in which you can type the new variable name **Age** into the **Result Variable** text box and give it a label if you want to. You are given the option to **Create the variable now** or **Paste the syntax into the syntax window**. In this case, leave the button where it is to create the variable now. The **Finish** button will become active and you should click it. Then you will be returned to the Data Editor window, where you will see the new variable **Age** with the ages 69, 67, 37 computed.

◆ If you wish, you may save these data for future reference by following the procedure described in section 2.7. Name the file **ages.sav**.

◆ Click **File** in the menu bar near the top of the Data Editor, then **Exit**.

Appendix 2: Exporting and Importing Excel Files

Sometimes the data you want to analyse has been entered into Excel spreadsheet files, especially as this is a widely used package in industry. It is a straightforward procedure to import the Excel file into SPSS or, alternatively, to save SPSS data to an Excel file. So that you have got an Excel file to import into SPSS, we will start by saving an SPSS file to Excel format.

EXPORTING DATA TO EXCEL

In chapter 2 you entered some data for **twina** and **twinb**. Either open that saved file now, called **twinsiq.sav**, download it from the book's web site, or type the data into a blank datasheet using the data editor.

◆ Click **File** in the menu bar and then click **Save As...** (as outlined in section 2.7). Don't just click **Save**, as this won't give you the chance to change the type of file to Excel.

◆ Now click the arrow on the right of the **Save in** (or **Look in** in SPSS 16) list box, and select a folder to save your file. If you want to save the data on a memory stick, then make sure **the Removable Disk (E:)** is selected. Type a new name into the box labelled **File name:** in this case we will call it **excel twins.**

◆ Now the important thing is to change the type of file, so use the black down arrow and look through the drop-down list to the right of **Save as type:** Select **Excel 97 and later (*.xls)** or, in SPSS 16, **Excel 97 through 2003 (*.xls)**. Make sure that there is a tick in the box labelled **Write variable names to spreadsheet,** if this box is not ticked you will lose the variable names and the Excel sheet will only have unlabelled numbers.

◆ If you want to export *all* of your variables then now you should click **Save**. If you don't want to export all variables, then click **Variables**, and in the new submenu box that appears uncheck the boxes next to the variables that you want to drop. Exit this submenu by clicking **Continue**. If you want to **Save value labels where defined instead of data values**, then click to tick this box, but bear in mind that it will save the labels such as "strongly disagree" but not the numbers such as "5" if you choose this, so it may or may not be desirable depending on what you intend to use the Excel file for. Leave it unchecked for the moment. Then click **Save**.

To see your Excel sheet, double-click the file name **excel twins.xls** in the location that you have just saved the file. Excel will open and you'll see your data.

Excel can only hold up to 256 columns of data, so if your data set has more variables than this, then you will need to reduce its size or split it into several files before exporting to Excel. There is, however, no limit on the number of cases, so data sets from thousands of participants are fine for exporting to Excel.

EXPORTING OUTPUT TO EXCEL (AND OTHER APPLICATIONS)

There are occasions when you may want to save your SPSS output in a different format from SPSS. For example, if you want to e-mail your output to someone who does not have the SPSS software, or is using a different version of it from yours, then you may want to send the file in a format such as HTML, Excel, or Word. You may also want to show your output on PowerPoint slides or PDF, and this is now possible.

◆ From the Output Viewer that you want to export, go to **File**, then **Export...** and the Export Output dialog box will open.

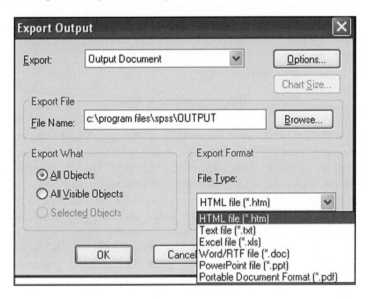

◆ Decide what you want to export and click one of the two radio buttons in the **Export What** (or, in SPSS 16, **Objects to Export**) group. If you choose the button next to **All Objects** (or, in SPSS 16, **All**), then everything will be exported (notes, logs, and so on). If you choose the button next to **All Visible Objects** (or, in SPSS 16, **All visible**), then only the output that you have left visible in the Output Viewer will be exported, and nothing else. To choose the button next to **Selected Objects** (or, in SPSS 16, **Selected**), you need first to select the object(s) that you want to export, and then if you choose this button, only those selected items will be exported. Similarly, using the drop-down menu next to **Export:** at the top of the dialog box, you can choose to export the whole output document, everything except the charts, or just the charts alone.

◆ In the **Export Format** (or, in SPSS 16, **Type**) box you can select the type of file you want the output saved as; HTML, Text, Excel, Word, PowerPoint, or PDF. All these options are available in SPSS versions 14, 15, and 16 apart from the PDF option, which is only in versions 15 and 16.

◆ The only remaining thing that you might want to change is the file format for the graphics (charts) to be exported to the new output file, which you do by clicking **Options** (or, in SPSS 16, by going to **Graphics** and scrolling down the **Type:** list) and then choosing the type you want. It will default to JPEG file format for the graphics unless you go into the options box and change it to TIF, BMP, and so on. The JPEG default is usually fine for most purposes.

♦ Click the **Browse** button to locate the folder where you want to save the new file, and name the file **output1.spo**.

Once you have clicked on **OK**, the output will be exported. Navigate to the folder where you saved the new file and double-click to open it so that you can check that the export procedure produced what you wanted. If you are going to do further calculations on the numbers in the output file, then it is probably best to save it to Excel, whereas if you want the formatting of the tables to look the same as in SPSS – for example, to put in the appendix to your report/thesis – then save the output to Word or PDF.

IMPORTING FROM EXCEL

♦ In the Excel sheet, check that the variable names are all in the top row. If data are in blocks with names lower down the sheet, then you'll need to rearrange them so that all the variable names are at the top, with data in the columns directly below them. Close the Excel file before you import it to SPSS.
♦ To import the Excel file into SPSS, start up SPSS and from a blank data editor sheet click **File**, **Open**, **Data...**, then locate the Excel file **excel twins.xls** using the **Look in:** box. You will *not* be able to see the Excel file you're looking for unless you change the **Files of type:** box to read **Excel (*.xls)** or **All Files (*.*)**. You should then be able to locate it. Click the file name and then click **Open**. The following box will appear, and you should click **OK** (or, in SPSS 16, **Continue**).

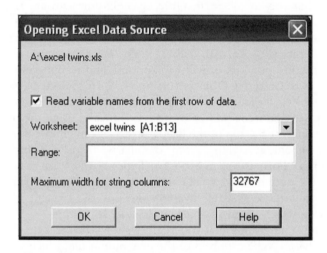

♦ The **twina** and **twinb** data will then appear in your data editor and you can save them as an SPSS file from here as usual (as described in section 2.7). You may then want to go into the Variable View and add Labels and Values if you need to.

One thing that you should bear in mind is that the data will only have been imported from the top Excel Worksheet 1. Some Excel files have multiple sheets, and you would have to click the arrow in the box to the right of **Worksheet** in the screenshot above to select a different one if there were several containing data. You would import each one, one at a time, into SPSS. It's really easiest if all of the data are on one Excel sheet to begin with, and you could do this using **C**opy and **P**aste in Excel.

When importing data from Excel, any long variable names will be shortened by SPSS if they exceed 64 characters. The long variable names will be used as variable labels, so your output should still be understandable even with abbreviated variable names. SPSS will keep a record in the SPSS Output Viewer of which, if any, variables were renamed.

References

Adherents.com. (n.d.). *Major religions of the world ranked by number of adherents.* Retrieved May 24, 2005, from http://www.adherents.com/Religions_By_Adherents.html.

Bickel, P. J., Hammel, E. A., & O'Connell, J. W. (1975). Sex bias in graduate admissions: Data from Berkeley. *Science, 187,* 398–404.

Cohen, J. (1992). A power primer. *Psychological Bulletin, 112,* 155–159.

Cohen, S., Lichtenstein, E., Prochaska, J. O., Rossi, J. S., Gritz, E. R., Carr, C. R., Orleans, C. T., Schoenbach, V. J., Biener, L., Abrams, D., DiClementi, C., & Curry, S. (1989). Debunking myths about self-quitting: Evidence from 10 prospective studies of persons who attempt to quit smoking by themselves. *American Psychologist, 44,* 1355–1365.

Colman, A. M. (1982). *Game theory and experimental games: The study of strategic interaction.* Oxford, UK: Pergamon.

Corston, R., & Colman, A. M. (1996). Gender and social facilitation effects on computer competence and attitudes toward computers. *Journal of Educational Computing Research, 14,* 171–183.

Fazio, R. H., Jackson, J. R., Dunton, B. C., & Williams, C. J. (1995). Variability in automatic activation as an unobtrusive measure of racial attitudes: A bona fide pipeline. *Journal of Personality and Social Psychology, 69,* 1013–1027.

Feller, W. (1968). *An introduction to probability theory and its applications* (3rd ed., Vol. 1). New York: Wiley.

Freedman, D., Pisani, R., Purves, R., & Adhikari, A. (1991). *Statistics* (2nd ed.). New York: Norton.

Hays, W. L. (2007). *Statistics* (6th ed.). Belmont, CA: Wadsworth.

Hovland, C. I., & Sears, R. R. (1940). Minor studies of aggression: VI. Correlation of lynchings with economic indices. *Journal of Psychology, 9,* 301–310.

Howell, D. C. (2008). *Fundamental statistics for the behavioral sciences* (6th ed.). Belmont, CA: Duxbury.

Huck, S. W. (2008). *Reading statistics and research* (5th ed.). Boston, MA: Allyn & Bacon.

Juel-Nielsen, N. (1965). Individual and environment: A psychiatric-psychological investigation of monozygous twins reared apart. *Acta Psychiatrica et Neurologica Scandinavica,* Monograph Supplement 183.

Knox, V. J., Morgan, A. H., & Hilgard, E. R. (1974). Pain and suffering in ischemia: The paradox of hypnotically suggested anesthesia as contradicted by reports from the "hidden observer". *Archives of General Psychiatry, 30,* 840–847.

Norman, G. R., & Streiner, D. L. (2008). *Biostatistics: The bare essentials* (3rd ed.). Toronto: B. C. Decker.

Norušis, M. J. (1993). *SPSS for Windows base system user's guide release 6.0.* Chicago, IL: SPSS Inc.

Pagano, R. R. (2007). *Understanding statistics in the behavioral sciences* (8th ed.). Belmont, CA: Wadsworth.

Simpson, E. H. (1951). The interpretation of interaction in contingency tables. *Journal of the Royal Statistical Society, Series B, 13(2)*, 238–241.

Spearman, C. (1904). "General intelligence", objectively determined and measured. *American Journal of Psychology, 15*, 201–293.

Thurstone, L. L. (1947). *Multiple-factor analysis: A development and expansion of The Vectors of Mind.* Chicago, IL: University of Chicago Press.

Universities Funding Council. (1993). *A report for the Universities Funding Council on the conduct of the 1992 research assessment exercise.* Bristol, UK: Author.

Index